A Contemporary Western Book Of The Dead

for our ancestors

Frontispiece by Ruth Kenyon

A Contemporary Western Book Of The Dead

Edited by
Charlotte Rodgers
and Lydia Maskell

Mandrake

Copyright © Charlotte Rodgers, Lydia Maskell and
Mandrake of Oxford 2012
1st Edition

All rights reserved. No part of this work may be reproduced or utilized in any form by any means electronic or mechanical, including *xerography, photocopying, microfilm,* and *recording,* or by any information storage system without permission in writing from the author.

Published by
Mandrake of Oxford
PO Box 250
OXFORD
OX1 1AP (UK)
ISBN 978-1-906958-04-6

Contents

Introduction
Charlotte Rodgers 6

Loved One
Nema 11

All a Do about Death
Josephine McCarthy 13

Clans For The Memory
Sarah Grimstone 33

Learning About Death
Nevill Drury 37

A Thoughtful Wake
Louis Martinie 62

Break On Through To The Other Side
Louise Hodgson 67

Death the Final Frontier
Sue Fox 72

The Bardo Thodol – Bon Voyage
John Power 75

You Only Live Twice
Ode bi Tola 117

On Speaking with the Dead:
The Cult of the Dead in Traditional Culture
Michael Clarke 120

Body
Mishlen Linden 137

The Great Western Hoax
Ode bi Tola 145

The Book of Gates:4 A prose arrangement
Mogg Morgan 168

Biographies of Contributors 179

Introduction

Charlotte Rodgers

I have been a magickal practitioner for over thirty years, and for most of that time I have worked with remnants of death which I have integrated, both in form and spirit, into magickal art. A combination of my age and certain life style choices mean that many people I have loved have died, and I have often been present during the process of death, or directly afterwards.

However when my mother died all these years of experience, study and practice slipped through my fingers. I was at a loss on how to honour her and also deal with my own grief within a spiritual context that I found both supportive and appropriate.

I am very privileged to have as friends and confidants, priests and teachers from traditions that are ancestor focused. As I found practical and emotional succour in their support and advice I decided to pull together a book of words and images from practitioners of various traditions who have worked practically with death and have wisdom and strength which they can communicate.

I contacted them with my project, giving the following, highlighted text for stimulus but no set criterion of format or structure, only asking for a contribution that came from the heart.

The ways they chose to participate varied as any expression of the

Little Scout Ariadne Xenou

individual and heartfelt would; this book contains dreams, rituals, history and experience.

There is mention of politics, race and class because these things impact on our lives and honouring the dead is honouring all aspects of our histories.

The words enclosed here are the words of our elders, and they are written to acknowledge, love and show respect for our dead and give support to the still living.

I was musing on Singapore in all its affluent glory still having shrines for the dead on every street corner during 'The Festival of the Hungry Ghosts'. Then I was musing on how the socially mobile of modern western society eschew death rites and grieving in the name of 'holding it together' and being progressive.

I thought of which civilisations are falling and which are rising again, and wondered whether acknowledging death and the ancestors is a vital part of a contemporary culture and maintaining personal identity within that culture.

I remember how my grieving father mourned for all the information he had relied on his deceased wife remembering, such as names of relatives, children and various in-family activities, which was now lost.

I recalled Michael Crichton's words 'If you don't know (your family's) history, then you don't know anything. You are a leaf that doesn't know it is part of a tree.'

THEN I *thought maybe someone should write about the cults of the ancestors and death, perhaps an anthology, perhaps cross relate experiences of loss to personal spirituality and magick and history.*

I know that years of working with the spirit world and goetic traditions, owning a lot of bones and communicating with the long dead didn't prepare me for working with the death of my mother.

What helped me was the advice of someone from a long tradition of working with the ancestors.

I think that collecting the experiences of spiritual practitioners in their working with grief and death is part of a living and necessary tradition that will give respect to the dead and strength, identity and support to our own personal spirituality.

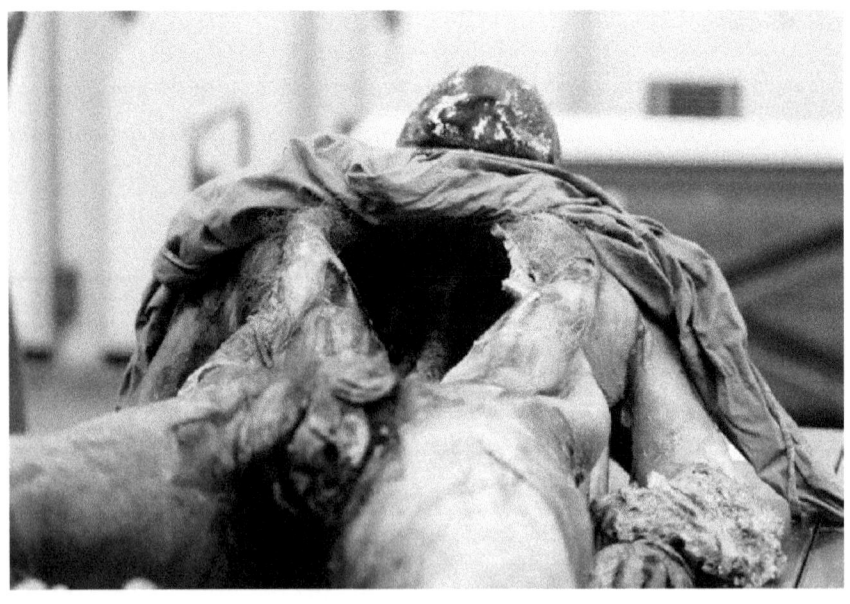

Sue Fox

Loved One
Nema

Turn off the machines.
I have to go on, you're holding me back,
turn off the machines.

I have to go on, to sever the thread
that binds me to earth
through my heart and my brain;
turn off the machines!

Have you not beheld me
as still as the grave,
with my spirit afar
and my body so cold?

Turn off the machines.

My time was suspended
both here and afar
while my shell and my spirit
learned wisdom anew
so that I might go on.

My time is completed

and now I return
to untangle the skein
of the silver cord's length.

But my life's line is captive
in tubes and machines.

Love is not binding,
love gives us freedom
not rooted in flesh,
it endures in the spirit.

You'll soon come to join me—
and as you do love me,
Turn off the machines

All a Do about Death

Josephine McCarthy

I was born into a large Catholic family with women who lived into their 90s and 100s (the men died young…ha!). Usually there are five generations alive at any one time and so at a very early age one became used to the usual round of wakes and births that is common to such a large and fertile line. Parts of my family were mystical Christians and ritualists, along with many priests, nuns and the odd smattering of bishops, so ritual and rites of passage were the norm. Finally, add to that the regular remembrances of my mother recalling her previous life as a male farmer and my great uncle who was convinced he was a reincarnation of Beethoven and you have a very strange but interesting upbringing!

As I grew up, the contradiction of Catholic heaven/hell/purgatory and reincarnation never really sunk in and I sort of accepted both as I sat and talked to the various dying relatives during my childhood. That was an important key for future magical sense: existence for a child is a chaotic harmony, and this is one of the strengths in magic.

My first real sense of death as a magician came with the death of my grandmother. She was ninety-two years of age and had been very bright and active until she sustained a foot injury that turned bad. She was hospitalized and we all took turns in visiting and providing a buffer for the madness of the gloomy Victorian hospital complete with its rattling pipes and scents of thymol.

Family Grave, Kifissa Ariadne Xenou

After she had been in for a week or so, I did an unscheduled visit just for the hell of it and found her sleeping. I planned to stop for only a few minutes as I had jobs to do. Something stopped me leaving. I just could not get out of my chair. My aunt arrived, then another, then my mother, my eldest sister, my niece, and soon she was surrounded by four generations of women. None of us could leave. We took turns instinctively touching her, providing energy and companionship. I felt a strong in-rush of magical power and minutes later she opened her eyes, looked past us all and died.

Days later, I smelled her scent in my house and understood. I said goodbye. Something shifted, something filled me but I did not understand what. I was too young, and had not enough formed knowledge to understand the processes that where happening. Her knowledge and wisdom was being 'jettisoned' and I was the nearest with the inner abiity to absorb it. Her gift to me unfolded over many years and still unfolds to this day: it is the sum of her experiences and the experiences of those who went before her. When I die, I too will cast off what I have learned and what skills I have acquired, and the nearest to me who has inner ability will pick it up.

Months after my Grandmother's death, I called out through the inner worlds for a teacher, for learning, for practical ways that I could be of service through death to my family and others. Nothing happened in that respect for a few more years and I was very frustrated that my call had not been answered, but in retrospect I had too many energetic responsibilities in nurturing and protecting my babies. If I had plunged into deeper esoteric mysteries, my children would have paid the price; I would have dragged their spirits with me as the spiritual and energetic bond between mother and child is tight and strong. I did not know that at the time but it was a good example of the wisdom that the door only opens when the time is right.

During that time I did encounter many deaths and many dead people. Friends, family, neighbours - it seemed like they were dropping like flies around me, and some refused to stop hanging around. Looking back, this was a time of important learning; I learned about the state of mind both before and after death, and how that state of mind can influence the quality of the passage. I also learned that people hang on to many things, the obvious belongings and people, but also self-image and the surviving family's recollection of that image.

People also hang grimly to religious doctrines, dogmas and fears; rather than assist a person, dogmas can often trap the spirit in a maze of confusion. I dealt with them one by one, learning on the hoof and trying not to make mistakes. I had a good esoteric teacher emerge at that time who would only point the way, but not actually carry me anywhere, which taught me to teach myself and stand on my own feet.

There were two deaths in my younger years that really taught me a great deal. They influenced my understanding of death and showed me how to work as a priestess within the realms of death. One was my father and the other was my nephew who was like a brother to me (we were the same age and I was raised partly by my sister).

When my father died I felt a strong sense of responsibility that I had to ensure his passage was smooth. He had been my spiritual and magical mentor through my childhood, and now it was my turn to give back. I knew about accessing the Underworld in vision, and I knew about the vision of the river of death from old stories, but I had never actually gone into death at that point.

I waited for twenty-four hours after he had died and then went on my first intentional visionary foray into death (as opposed to blindly stumbling in by accident). The vision of death that I knew about from childhood was the vision of the desert with the river of death that flows through it. Many years later I began to understand that it is a part of the inner pattern known as the Tree of Life.

My father was standing at the side of the river of death; he was waiting for something and seemed a little bit confused. I walked up to him and immediately began asking him how he was, did he realize what had happened etc. He stared at me for a moment before telling me that he had no idea who I was. I was shocked and upset: I had imagined a wonderful tearful reunion after death and he being proud of me for walking into death while still alive. I needed that parental pride.

However he didn't recognize me and I was totally unprepared for that. A being that was nearby, helping others, heard my distress and came over. The being explained to me that we often do not look like our living image when we appear in the inner worlds; we can take on many appearances, some of them not even remotely human like. The being also advised me that I should not try to explain to my father who I was, that it is better that he begins to let go straight away in death.

I ignored the being's advice and explained to my dad who I was and why I looked different. It took a while to convince him but eventually he caved in and we began to chat. While we chatted, I walked him over the bridge, which is an important step in death and let him ramble about his memories, some which shocked me.

I went back and forth in vision to be with him over a series of ten days. By the seventh day he had forgotten who I was and who he was in his life. He had gotten to a place where he had let go of his old life and was preparing for the long journey that would eventually take him back into life. I continued to go into the death vision until he no longer appeared: I wanted to learn as much as I could from direct experience. I connected with the many beings that worked in death and pestered them with endless questions.

After that, I began to go into death on a fairly regular basis, helping people who were stuck and generally trying to observe the process as much as I could. It completely changed how I viewed death and dying. I had always been told that there was life after death, but to see it for myself was very important to my learning process. I also didn't have to wait long to get confirmation that it was not all in my head. Information was given to me in the death vision that left me with no doubt that what I was experiencing was real.

The second death that taught me a great deal was the death of my nephew. He had died in his sleep at the tender age of thirty and was not found for quite a long time. As soon as I found out I went in to the death vision and found him weeping at the side of the river. He would not move at all. I tried to get him to walk over the bridge, but he would not budge. I tried to get him to drink the water of the river, which would basically wipe his memory, but he would not. I went back and forth in the death vision for three days and he would not budge an inch. He also appeared in the strangest way. He looked out of focus, like an image breaking up. I asked one of the death beings, one of the helpers, and they told me that my nephew appeared that way because he was literally breaking up: he was decomposing at a fast rate.

On the fourth day, I knew I had to do something. My nephew's distress was so profound; he had begun to affect his mother, my sister. We are both very strong empaths and she was unconsciously taking on his suffering: her grief was profound, which is understandable, but the pain she was suffering was more than her own; she was carrying her son's pain also. I did what I always do when I run into a magical blank wall – I went to ask mummy for help.

I went in vision to the Underworld Dark Goddess and asked her what I should do. She told me to bring him to her. I left and went straight into the death vision, not thinking to ask her exactly how I should get him to her from the death vision if I couldn't get him to go anywhere. So when I got there, I realized I didn't know what to do so I 'winged it.' The Underworld is down right? So I grasped hold of him and imagined a hole opening up in the desert and we both tumbled down it into the cave of the Dark Goddess. I stood him before her and I was told to go and wait at a distance.

I watched as she talked to him very gently and kindly; I had never seen her speak with such tenderness before. He was crying and emptying out his pockets, which were full of letters, bills and the like. I couldn't hear what he was saying but as soon as his pockets were empty, her hair grew out in front of her and whipped around him in a tornado type action. It all happened so fast and he was gone: she pulled him into herself with her hair. I was shocked and fascinated all at once. I was told very abruptly to leave, which I did. Later, I went and asked her about it and all she would tell me was that he was asleep within her. After that point, he never appeared in the death vision again.

These experiences and others had a profound effect on my magical work that continues to unfold. The intricacies of the soul's path from conception through to death and then back into birth again weave in and out of the inner tides that flow through our world. I became fascinated by the deeper implications of death upon our families and societies, and also by the beings that exist alongside us through these various transitions. Death work, along with exorcism became a major part of my magical work for many years, and later, a major part of my teaching.

The western societies in general seemed to have lost all sense of the needs of the dead and dying, focusing their attention instead on the bereaved and their path to emotional recovery. That is all well and good, but what about the dead person? Christianity essentially took away our understanding of death as a natural component of life, and instead turned it into a bizarre final exam, which if you failed, you were doomed to an existence of horror. At best, it led us to believe that it was the end, nada… the full stop on consciousness.

I began to study various ancient texts on death and the realm of death. Once the dogma and dressing was stripped from the texts, what was left was interestingly similar and corresponded very closely to the experiences I had gone through as I escorted people through the death vision. The more I worked from a visionary point of view, the clearer things became in the understanding of where everything fitted and why. I worked closely with the Tree of Life, not as a series of pathways and spheres, but as a landscape with the Abyss at one end and the river of death at the other and birth being Malkuth in the middle. I began to see how the path through death sometimes took an aware person through the realm of the ancient library, where the knowledge they had acquired in life could be held in an inner space so that others could partake of that knowledge. This holding of knowledge is the source of ancestral wisdom that can be accessed by working with ancestors through ritual and vision.

The deeper I plunged into the Abyss, the Underworld and the realm of death, the more certain dogmas made a peculiar sort of sense. The first one that hit me was the concept of purgatory. When I was growing up, my father called purgatory "God's waiting room'. The church's view was that it was a place where the soul could prepare for heaven. During a visit to the realm of death, I was standing at the side of the river watching some people cross the bridge. Many stood around refusing to move, and some others did not even see the bridge. Some were fading in and out, as if they were not quite dead, and others did not understand that they were actually dead.

This was the area of death where the spirit could still interact with the living world. Those who could figure out how to use their imaginations could pass back and forth in their minds between the realms. Others stayed in this holding space purposely, passing back and forth between the realms of life and death, watching over and helping their families. Then the penny dropped; this was God's waiting room! Strip off all the dogma and religious dressing and what you get is a state of consciousness whereby the spirit slowly lets go of the life just lived and moves forward further into death slowly until they are ready to cross the bridge.

The second penny that dropped was the understanding of why the path of magical training at its deepest level insists upon the strict discipline of the body, and the ability to fast and put the needs and wants of the body to one side. With that amount of discipline, when the spirit has crossed the desert of death and arrived at the river, the burning thirst can be ignored. Only a tiny sip of the river water is drunk, thus allowing the adept to retain all of their accumulated knowledge.

The water strips the spirit of all memory and understanding so that it can then continue through death without being held back by emotional or physical bonds. The more magical or spiritual knowledge a person has, the more they understand the process they are going through and can take informed decisions. If they wish to just let go, they chose to drink plenty. If they are on a path of service where they need to retain memories and information, then only a tiny drop is drunk, just to help them let go of deep emotional bonds or issues. If the adept has learned the mysteries properly, then they will not need to drink of the water as they will have learned the path of death within life and will not be attached to anything; instead they will simply wash their face.

The other big revelation I picked up regarding the death mysteries was the secret of the mountain. Beyond the river is a great mountain that must be climbed. I noticed many times as I worked in the realm of death that the mountain often changed in size according to who was climbing it at that particular time. On the occasions that I had climbed up the mountain with someone, like my father for example, I noticed that there were lots of voices, almost like recitations and arguments, but I could never quite catch what they said. Then one day I was reading a Jewish text (don't ask which one because I cannot remember) that mentioned the mountains that we create for our spirits to climb are built from our dogmas, studies and theories. It's basically the bullshit that we surrounded our spirits with in life, bullshit that had dug deep into our unconscious and needed to be overcome. Then the bits fell into place and made sense. The next time I journeyed into death to help someone, I paid more attention to what I heard as I climbed the mountain with them. It was right; the spirit I walked with truly struggled as they walked up the side of the mountain.

I think it is important to point out that what we as living people see, feel and hear in the death vision is not what the dead person sees: it is our brain's way of making sense of the energies that the spirit encounters as it passes through various strands of power. The pictures that we see, i.e. river, mountain, desert etc are images that have been built up over thousands of years and have become, from a visionary point of view, well trodden paths that our consciousness is drawn to. Where the original idea for those images comes from I have no idea. I just find it curious that such images pop up all over the world in various versions.

For me as a magician it has been a very important journey to work in death; it is one of the most powerful things that happens to us, and how we pass into death seems to have a direct impact not only on ourselves, but the land and beings around us. I feel that with greater understanding of death, its process and the way it challenges us to put our learning in to practice, it deepens our relationship with the power of Divine Consciousness (as opposed to deity) and how we interact with that power. Engaging in death work takes us away from the question of what happens to us after death and the accompanying feeling of helplessness, and brings us to a more mature understanding of this powerful transitional step in our existence.

I have included below a version of the death vision that I use. Those magicians who are involved in the Western Mysteries, Egyptian Mysteries and Etruscan magick will recognize some of the images within this vision.

Death Vision

The best way to work with this vision is to record it and play it back to yourself as you sit in meditation. Do not lie down to listen to this vision in case you fall asleep.

Light a candle, sit down and close your eyes. See the flame with your inner vision and as you look at the flame, see the flame fall down into the earth and you are drawn to follow it. You and the flame fall down and down, deep into the underworld, leaving the surface world behind.

As you fall through the darkness, the flame falls ahead of you and you follow it as you fall together through the underworld. You land in a cave, landing on soft sand and the flame waits beside you. In the cave is a river that flows through the darkness and you call out through the darkness for the boatman.

A light appears on the river in the darkness and a slow boat appears with an old man rowing it. A small lamp holds a flame at the head of the boat and he rows towards you. Once he pulls over to you, put your hand in your pocket and pull out a coin, which you give to him. He helps you into the boat and he rows off down the river, which passes through dark tunnels that run deep in the underworld.

Sunlight appears ahead and the boat emerges out in a landscape with mountains to your left and a desert to your right. He pulls over on the right hand side of the river bank and waits for you to get out.

As you get out you become aware of people walking towards the river from the desert and of people sitting beside the river. Many seem confused and shocked: some are not sure what has happened to them or where they are. Stand among them and call the name of the dead person that you seek. Keep calling until they walk towards you or identify themselves somehow.

Once you have them, look them over to ensure that no parasites are attached to them and if there are, remove them and put them in the river. Once they are clean, turn them to face the river and show them a bridge that spans it. The bridge is usually guarded by two beings.

Walk them to the bridge and tell them that they must cross the bridge and walk into death. If they resist, you must explain to them that there is nowhere else for them to go and that they really need to step forward onto this new path. If they still will not move, ask the help of the angelic beings. If they come to help, do not be surprised if they change their appearance: they are dressing in a way that the dead person expects them to look; they may appear as a relative or religious figure. The angelic beings choose the image that is the most likely to have a positive effect on the dead person.

Once they have crossed the bridge, walk them to the mountains and talk to them about letting go of their life, their belongings, relationships and connections. You need to help them understand that their previous life has now gone and that world no longer exists for them: this total letting go allows the spirit to free itself and prepare for the next experience. If they do not let go, they will carry issues, fears and connections with them into their next life, which is nearly always an unhealthy thing for the soul.

As you approach the mountain, look for a pathway up the side of it that you can both walk. The mountain is composed of their prejudices that are deeply embedded, often religious, so as you climb the mountain with them, they will often hear religious recitation or lots of discussion.

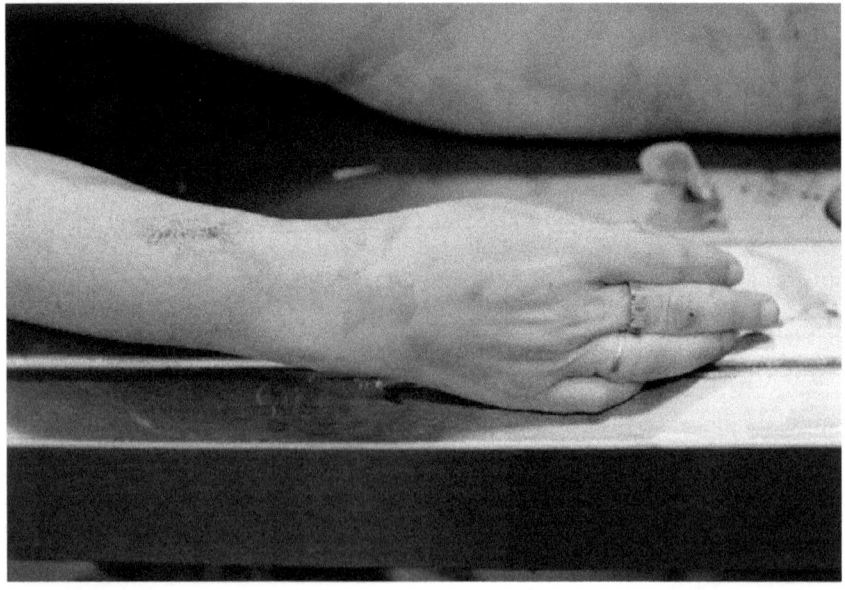

Sue Fox

It is the spirit's structure it has created for itself throughout life to cope with and understand power and energy.

The higher you climb, the quieter the voices will become until you reach the top and it is silent. Angelic beings will be waiting at the top and they will ask the dead person to lie down and rest. As they lie down, the angelic beings begin to sing them to sleep and stroke them: the soul and spirit become disconnected at this point, and the soul goes through renewal before tumbling back into life.

At this point your job is now done but you cannot go back down the way you came: energetically that would too exhausting and would put too heavy a strain on you. Look beyond the angelic beings and you will see a deep mist. Walk towards the mist and step into it with the intention of stepping into the void.

Stepping through the mist you find yourself in nothing and a silence settles around you. This is the void, the place where all power comes from and returns to. Be still in this place until you are ready to move on. When you are ready, think about the place where you started the vision and think of the flame. With that intention step forward and you will pass out of the void and find yourself stepping through the flame back into the room where you first started.

When you are ready, put out the candle flame.

© 1998-2010 Josephine McCarthy

Jai Maha Ma
A Greater Feast
A Rite of Passage

By Nema

"A feast for fire and a feast for water;
a feast for life and a greater feast for death!"
Liber AL vel Legis Ch.II v.41

As I write these words, my husband's mother lies dying. She was a formidable woman, a widow with three sons, a partner in a market research company and a person both generous with her gifts and devastating with her commentary.

Although Anita was born and raised a Jew, she didn't practice a religion. She did practice selective traditions, however, and delighted in the company of children. This ritual is shaping itself as I reach out to her astrally from my home and in the guise of prayer in her care facility.

There are times when magick must be done invisibly and effectively in crowded conditions. A good mask to use is prayer, particularly during deaths, births and weddings. Ceremony eases transitions while it transmits a power to the participants, a power called Tao-Teh, prana, shakti, mana, grace, etc.

When possible, have flowers in the room, preferably alive and potted. Since candles and oxygen supplies might not peacefully coexist, use one or more mirrors to reflect light on the ceiling, preferably natural light from a window. If placing a mirror is impossible, visualize light filling the room, soft and shadowless.

When the 'congregation' (including the dying Goer) consists of magi, then the ritual can be done aloud, with gestures, dance, chanting, and other spiritual aids. When your companions are strangers or are known to you as uninitiate, then speak silently in your mind and imagine your movements, sounds, and surroundings. To avoid conversation, close your eyes, fold your hands, and move your lips silently (optional).

The rite begins.

[You hang suspended in a pearl gray mist,
facing toward the Goer but not straining for an image. You declare:]

'This is a time that is not a time
In a place that is not a place
On a day that is not a day
In a space that is not a space—
Between the worlds, and beyond.'

[Envision or look at the Goer's head,
listen to his/her breathing,
and call:]
Guardians of the watchtower of the East, the powers of Air, clarify the mind of (Goer's name) in preparation for a new way of seeing and understanding.

[Envision or look at the Goer's arms and chest while invoking:]

Guardians of the watchtower of the South, the powers of Fire, lead (Goer's name) heart and strength to surrender this phase of existence.

[Envision or look at the Goer's abdomen and hips, then say:]

Guardians of the watchtower of the West, the powers of Water, flow the peace and relief of completion into (Goer's name) soul and emotions.

[Envision or look at the Goer's legs and feet, while summoning:]

Guardians of the watchtower of the North, the powers of Earth, establish the unity of matter and time in (Goer's name) knowledge and senses.

So mote it be.

[Silently, astrally, call his/her name three times,
identify yourself, then say:]

It's good to see you and to be with you. Soon you'll leave this material world and step into mystery. Gather yourself to a point behind and above your eyes; this is your best gateway.

When you feel yourself losing feeling in your hands and feet, in your arms and legs, in your trunk and head, go to that point and leave on your last breath. Soar up and out into freedom when you know that your time has come.

For now we wait together patiently. There is no hurry, there is no delay. Rest in the love that surrounds you.

[As the Goer slips into sleep, invoke the godform(s) of your choice, if any. Example:]

(Chanted, silently or aloud:)

ISIS, ASTARTE, DIANA, HECATE, DEMETER, KALI, INANNA (x 3)

WE ALL COME FROM THE GODDESS, AND TO HER WE SHALL RETURN, LIKE A DROP OF RAIN FLOWING TO THE OCEAN.

PAN, WOTAN, BAPHOMET, CERNUNNOS, OSIRIS (x 3)

WE ALL COME FROM THE SUN GOD, AND TO HIM WE SHALL RETURN, LIKE A SPARK OF FLAME SOARING TO THE HEAVENS.

(Spoken, silently or aloud:) HAIL, LADY NUIT, GREAT NIGHT SKY, BLESS (Goer's name) IN HIS/HER DYING, OPENING HIS/HER SOUL TO YOUR SPLENDID GLORY, EMBRACING HIM/HER IN YOUR OMNIPRESENT LOVE.

SO MOTE IT BE.

HAIL, LORD HADIT, POINT AND SINGULARITY, BLESS (Goer's name) IN HIS/HER DYING, DRAWING HIM/HER INTO YOUR INFINITE WILL.

SO MOTE IT BE.

Optional hymn/verse (poet unknown)

L'Envoi

Under a wide and starry sky,
Dig the grave and let me lie.
Glad did I live and glad do I die,
I lay me down with a will.
And this be the verse ye grave for me:
Here he lies where he wants to be.
Home is the sailor, home from the sea,
And the hunter home from the hill.

Clans For The Memory

Sarah Grimstone

Hmmmm, why the hell would I want to get in contact with my ancestors? On my mother's side they ranged from the self obsessed to ones with an unhealthy sexual attraction to kids. I think I'd rather leave the buggers (excuse the pun) where they are thank you very much. It doesn't help that they're German.

And if I go further back on the Frau Holke tree, I find a group of Italian Jews who were extremely wealthy and had a penchant for inbreeding. Being extremely wealthy automatically makes you a card carrying member of the Almighty Arsehole Club in my book, so no; you can keep your ancestors - I'd probably get more sense out of my toaster.

I was born a McVey, which according to history were a bunch of Royalist nutjobs who were a sept of the Clan Maclean; a sept is basically a small clan which is looked after by a much larger clan, who had bigger clubs and probably a better supply of woad or something.

Some of the McVey's went to Ireland and then on to America to become policemen in New York, well that's according to the Simpsons, so it's probably true.

The thing is, whenever I hear Scottish or Irish music, I get all patriotic and want to start hating the English. I can jig for hours and it's the only music that can move my soul; not that I admit it in public; I pretend it's the Foo Fighters or Muse that does that.

I also have an obsession with pickles and chunks of pork, not just a passing thing, an actual craving. I've been heard to say, 'you can keep your cake, but offer me a gherkin and I'll give you a blow job!'

This has made me think, that although the thought of invoking my ancestors is anathema to me, they are in me. My genetic memory rises up and shouts, 'Och hen, come and have a wee dance!' Or 'Essen sie ein schnitzel!', I can't help it, it feels like being raped by your own cells.

So maybe I should get over myself and accept who I am, the next

Saints/Modern Icons Ariadne Xenou

chapter in the great Holke/McVey continuum. I don't have to like my ancestors, but maybe by giving them a few minutes thought, it may enrich my life, and make me feel part of a huge tree stretching back through the ages. The tree will probably have Dutch elm disease though.

So to end my rather glib addition to Charlotte's lovely book, I will quote my opener for when I did stand up comedy, it seems rather apt.

"Hi, my name's Sarah Grimstone, I'm half German and half Scottish – that makes me a really well organized and efficient alcoholic.'

See? My ancestors aren't really dead; they are sneaking around in my body waiting for inappropriate moments to well up and force me to enjoy pork bellies, sword dancing and copious amounts of booze.

I'm not entirely sure if that's actually a good thing or not, ask my doctor.

Lady of the Roses Ariadne Xenou

Learning About Death

Nevill Drury

When it comes to the issue of death and a possible afterlife there are only two options that ultimately confront us – either we are going to survive it or we won't. If the scientific materialists and sceptics are right and consciousness is a by-product of the brain, there is ultimately nothing further to be said – the final passage into death will simply be an individual transition into nothingness, perhaps assisted by naturally occurring chemicals in the brain that kick in during the final stages of the dying process to provide a natural, protective 'high'. However, if the sceptics are wrong and there *is* some form of life after death it will mean that individual consciousness has survived the death of the brain – the organ we have automatically assumed is vital to awareness. We would then have to embrace the quite radical suggestion that the living brain does not actually *create* consciousness but only *mediates* it while the human organism is alive and intact, and that consciousness itself – that is to say, our individual awareness – moves into a new domain during the transition through death.

Until relatively recently assertions about the post-mortem fate of human consciousness – the vital essence, or 'soul' – were presumed to be the exclusive domain of faith-based religious institutions. In the West this has meant looking to Christianity, Islam and Judaism for answers relating to the afterlife. Of the three, Judaism is probably the least helpful – Jewish sacred texts and literature have relatively little to say about what happens after death. The Torah and the Talmud focus primarily on earthly life and the need to fulfil one's duties to God and one's fellow human beings. There are vague conceptions about re-connecting with one's ancestors after death and references in some texts to the shadowy realm of Sheol as the home of the soul. The wicked and unrighteous, meanwhile, are likely to find themselves in the fiery pit of Gehinnom. Christianity and Islam are both resurrection-based religions that embrace the notion of a Last Judgement or Final Day that ultimately determines the fate of the soul for all eternity. And although there are minor differences between Islam and the Catholic and Protestant traditions in Christianity the bottom line is that the righteous will dwell in Paradise in the presence of God, while wicked non-believers who have turned away from the gift of 'salvation' will be consigned to the punishment of Hell forever.

In a greatly simplified sense this is what the mainstream Western religious traditions have to offer us. Especially with regard to Christianity and Islam, it becomes crucial to have *faith* in what they are proposing and commit ourselves exclusively to their cause in order to be 'saved'. In the often heated debates currently being waged between militant atheists like Richard Dawkins and Christopher Hitchens on the one hand, and a range of fundamentalist Christians on the other, the afterlife is either non-existent (because consciousness ceases with the death of the brain) or consists of a form of Heaven or Hell based entirely on one's religious allegiance and commitment. But is it possible that there is another way of engaging in this important debate? Could there be a place for what we might call 'evidence-based spirituality' as an alternative to materialistic atheism and religious fundamentalism? This would mean adopting spiritual perspectives based not on established religious texts and doctrines but on new and current scientific evidence related to the dying process. Speaking personally, I think that the scientific research into near-death experiences – a body of systematic consciousness-data gathered now for more than thirty years – goes some way to providing a substantial alternative not only to faith-based beliefs about the afterlife but also the reductionist perspectives of the militant atheists.

The challenge of death

Exploring the experience of death is perhaps the greatest remaining challenge in the study of human consciousness. From a theoretical perspective at least, knowing more about death would not only teach us more about what to expect when we die, but also how we should live our lives on the planet now. We are indeed fortunate that the scientific and medical investigation of the near-death experience is beginning to provide useful insights into the possible nature of death itself. Thanatology – the study of death and the dying process – is now a major realm of enquiry in the study of human consciousness and one of its most significant findings is that emerging perspectives on death threaten to overturn current widespread assumptions relating to the mind / body relationship.

We usually define death as the absence of all visible signs of life – there is no heartbeat or respiration in the human organism and all brain-wave activity has ceased (any EEG monitoring of electrical brain impulses would register as zero). To all intents and purposes such a person is clinically dead. The issues we are considering here relate to the experiences of people who have been pronounced medically to be clinically dead – and whose memory circuits are therefore totally inoperative – and yet have revived to recount their often mystical and visionary experiences. Because these people didn't finally die after all, their visionary episodes are referred to as *near-death experiences*, or NDEs. They nevertheless provide us with the best scientifically based data on what may happen to us when we die, and to that extent represent a potential meeting ground between the worlds of science and spirituality.[1]

Exploring the near-death experience

The term 'near-death experience' was coined in 1975 by the American philosopher and teacher, Dr Raymond Moody, author of the best-selling book *Life After Life*. Moody had begun collecting anecdotal accounts of near-death incidents in 1972 and his book was based on 150 accounts from people who contacted him as a result of articles he had written or lectures he had given on this topic.

The NDE by definition involves the return from apparent clinical death to waking consciousness and as such can be considered a substantially contemporary phenomenon because it has been greatly assisted by advances in medical technology.[2] It is only because the techniques of medical resuscitation and life-support are now so sophisticated that we have a burgeoning literature which describes the accounts of people who have seemingly 'died' and yet lived to tell the tale. These accounts, and the scientific and medical commentaries accompanying them, provide a new focus for the philosophical issues of mind and body in the debate over the nature of human consciousness and the 'soul'.

Among the first modern accounts anticipating the NDE studies was the work of Swiss geologist, Professor Albert Heim, who collected data on the experiences of people who had nearly died in mountain-climbing accidents or warfare. Heim's writings were translated in the 1970s by Russell Noyes and Ray Kletti, and included instances where people faced with the prospect of imminent death experienced a panoramic life-review or heard transcendental music. Also preceding the more recent NDE literature were the findings of Dr Karlis Osis, a Latvian-born parapsychologist based in New York, who conducted a survey of deathbed visionary experiences. Osis despatched questionnaires to 10,000 physicians and nurses and received 540 responses. On the basis of these he published a book titled *Death-bed Observations by Physicians and Nurses* in 1961 and followed it with a more substantial volume, *At the Hour of Death*, in 1977. In these works Osis noted that terminal subjects often experienced periods of bliss and spiritual peace prior to death. Some also saw apparitions of deceased relatives or friends coming to greet them, and seemed to realize intuitively that these figures were about to help them through the transition of death itself.

However it was Raymond Moody's book, *Life After Life*, that became the principal catalyst and inspiration for others interested in NDEs, and there have been several systematic research studies of the phenomenon since then – in the United States, Britain and Australia. Among those who have played a prominent role in this work are Dr Kenneth Ring from the University of Connecticut (co-founder of the International Association for Near-Death Studies – IANDS – in the United States), his British colleague Dr Margot Grey, world-famous thanatologist Dr Elisabeth Kubler-Ross, Australian psychologist Dr Cherie Sutherland, Dr Michael Sabom from Emory University in Atlanta and Dr Bruce Greyson from the University of Virginia. British researchers Dr Sam Parnia and Dr Peter Fenwick and the Dutch cardiologist Dr Pim van Lommel – who are currently pioneering a new direction in near-death research – believe that monitoring cardiac arrest patients in particular provides us with the most pertinent insights into key aspects of the dying process.

Kenneth Ring's *Life at Death*, published in 1980, was the first scientific study of NDEs and was based on over 100 interviews with medical subjects who had survived near-death. Ring's pioneering volume summarised the results of a systematic investigation conducted in several hospitals in Connecticut and Maine. His survey described what happens at the threshold of death, including the frequency of NDEs and the manner in which the patients almost died – whether through illness, accident or attempted suicide. Ring followed this publication in 1984 with *Heading Toward Omega*, a lucid overview of the spiritual implications of the NDE. Ring and his international colleagues have described the 'core' NDE in broadly the same way: an 'altered state' of feeling (peace, joy, serenity etc.); a sense of movement or separation from the body (an aerial perspective on the body, generally heightened awareness); a journey through a tunnel towards either a transcendent dimension or some other, more tangible realm (a celestial valley, garden or city), the experience of light and beauty; encounters in the spirit world with deceased relatives, spirits or 'guides' and sometimes religious figures like Jesus or 'God'. They have also sought to evaluate the impact such visionary experiences have had on the lives of the NDE subjects themselves. Ring, Grey, Greyson and Sutherland have all come to the conclusion that the 'core' NDE is largely *invariant*, that it occurs in much the same form – though not with all the characteristics present in every individual case – irrespective of nationality, social class, age, sex, educational level or occupation. What is highly significant about this finding is that the core aspects of the NDE are comparatively constant irrespective of whether that person is a religious believer, atheist or agnostic: in other words, the NDE seems to be pointing towards characteristics of human consciousness rather than towards a wide variety of disjointed or divergent sensory experiences such as one might expect if the experience was purely hallucinatory. To this extent the NDE seems to be telling us about the process of dying itself and the various stages or transitions of human perception which might occur beyond bodily death.

Once again we have the difficult issue of body, mind and spirit to resolve: during a NDE, is the subject projecting consciousness beyond the confines of the physical body and, if so, how is such a thing possible? In Kenneth Ring's *Life at Death* survey, 97.4 per cent of core NDE experiencers felt that their bodies were light or absent; 94.6 per cent found their sense of time either expanded or absent, and 81.8 per cent experienced space 'as either extended, infinite or absent'. As Ring observes: 'For most respondents, body, time and space simply disappear – or, to put it another way, they are no longer meaningful constructs.'[3]

Such aspects of the NDE, as one would expect, have proved problematic for reductionist researchers keen on explaining away the phenomenon as illusory or hallucinatory. Among the most commonly reported 'explanations' from this camp are that NDEs are delusory experiences which result from temporal lobe seizure or loss of oxygen as one approaches death; that they are simply re-enactments of the birth process; that they are caused by anaesthetic drugs, and that they are the symptoms of psychological factors related to the likely onset of death.

Here is a summary of these explanations, with comments on their relevance in each case:

Hallucinations and delusions: Dr Michael Sabom was particularly impressed in his medical survey by the ability of autoscopic (out-of-the-body / self-observing) NDE subjects to report details of actual events (medical equipment, surgical procedures, real conversations) from a detached and elevated position. 'The details of these perceptions were found to be accurate in all instances where corroborating evidence was available.' Dr Sabom also reported that some NDE subjects experienced hallucinations during their coma states and were able to distinguish clearly between the two categories of perception.[4]

Temporal lobe seizure: Seizures deriving from the temporal lobes (or non-motor portions) of the brain involve sensory distortions of the size or location of objects close by, and sometimes a feeling of detachment from the environment. They are also characterized by feelings of fear and loneliness and visual or auditory hallucinations. On the other hand, many NDE subjects report accurate, undistorted perceptual fields and may feel elated or relaxed about their dissociated condition.

Loss of oxygen in the brain: Under normal circumstances, if the oxygen supply to the brain is reduced, this produces a state of mental confusion and cognitive dysfunction. This is certainly not characteristic of the core NDE, which is often described by subjects as profoundly real and perceptually coherent. Some subjects suffering from brain hypoxia (oxygen loss) – for example, mountain climbers who have trekked in rarefied atmospheres – find they experience an onset of laziness and irritability, and they may also find it difficult to remember what they were thinking or doing at the time. Many NDE subjects, on the other hand, are so awed by the clarity and detail of their experiences that they remember them for many years afterwards.

Reliving the birth process: If NDEs, which are characterized by feelings of passing through a tunnel towards light, are somehow related to the normal birth process, then people born by Caesarian section should not experience them. Dr Susan Blackmore – a well known sceptic in relation to the NDE data – gave a questionnaire to 254 people, of whom 36 had been born by Caesarian section. 'Both groups reported the same proportion of out-of-the-body and tunnel experiences,' she has written. 'It could be that the experiences are based on the *idea* of birth in general, but this drastically weakens the theory.' [5]

Anaesthetic drugs: There are several cases of NDE subjects who received no anaesthetic drugs during their hospitalization, so this explanation, if indeed it is one at all, would not apply in many instances. While it is true that some dissociative anaesthetics like ketamine hydrochloride (Ketalar) may produce an experience in which one's consciousness appears distinct from the body and there may also be an awareness of journeying through tunnels in space, Ketalar is not widely used in human medical treatment and is now for the most part restricted to veterinary practice. In general, drug-induced hallucinations seem to be markedly different from NDEs. Dr Sabom notes that drug experiences are 'highly variable and idiosyncratic' and 'markedly different from NDEs, which always show a remarkable degree of invariance'.

Psychological factors: One psychological view of NDEs is that the experience derives from 'depersonalisation'. This theory, advanced by Noyes and Kletti (who translated the Heim material) argues that the ego has to protect itself from impending death and thus creates a perceptual scenario which supports the feeling of continuing mental integration. As Dr Noyes has said: 'As an adaptive pattern of the nervous system it alerts the organism to its threatening environment while holding potentially disorganizing emotion in check.' Dr Sabom rejects this view as a blanket explanation of the NDE because there were subjects in his survey who had out-of-the-body NDEs without being aware psychologically of any likelihood of imminent death. Some of these were subjects who experienced loss of waking consciousness without warning, due to a stoppage of the heart. Also, as Dr Margot Grey has indicated, 'depersonalization' is unable to account for NDE subjects who have claimed to have had meetings with relatives who had recently died but whom the NDE subject *did not know at the time had died*. Here the NDE subject would learn of the relative's actual death only after recovering from the NDE: the expectation prior to the NDE would be that the person concerned was still alive.

What happens during a NDE ?

It may be worthwhile at this point to quote a few brief but characteristic examples of what NDE subjects actually report, because their testimonies are our starting point and they provide insights into the processes involved:

I felt as though I was looking down at myself, as though I was way out here in space... I felt sort of separated. It was a wonderful feeling. It was marvellous. I felt very light and didn't know where I was...And then I thought that something was happening to me... This wasn't night. I wasn't dreaming... And then I felt a wonderful feeling as if I was out in space. *I felt myself being separated: my soul drawing apart from the physical being, was drawn upward seemingly to leave the earth and to go upward where it reached a greater Spirit with whom there was a communion, producing a remarkable new relaxation and deep security.*

I went into this kind of feeling of ecstasy and just started moving outward energetically... and then I experienced a replay of all of my life... from my birth to the actual operation...it was like it was on a fast-forward video...people, places, everything...

It is not uncommon for NDE subjects to report contact with deceased relatives or friends. In Dr Sabom's survey of 116 NDE subjects, 28 described encounters with other personages. One of Dr Sabom's case studies involved a seriously injured soldier, and his account of his deceased colleagues is intriguingly matter-of-fact:

I came out of my body, and perceived me laying on the ground with three limbs gone...What makes this so real was that the thirteen guys that had been killed the day before, that I had put in plastic bags, were right there with me. And more than that, during the course of that month of May, my regular company lost forty-two dead. All forty-two of those guys were there. They were not in the form we perceive the human body, and I can't tell you what form they were in because I don't know. But I know they were there. I felt their presence. We communicated without talking with our voices. There was no sympathy, no sorrow. They were already where they were. They didn't want to go back. That was the basic tone of our communication...that we were all happy right where we were. [6]

NDE research among the blind

In a potentially highly significant research study, Kenneth Ring and his colleague Sharon Cooper have recently explored near-death experiences among the blind. This research is important because if it could be demonstrated that blind people have their sight restored to them during a near-death experience the entire relationship between body, mind and spirit would obviously have to re-assessed.

In 1997 Ring and Cooper approached eleven national and regional American associations for the blind in order to locate individuals who had experienced near-death experiences (NDEs) or out-of-the-body experiences (OOBEs). Forty-six individuals were subsequently screened for the research study, of whom 31 qualified for inclusion. They included 20 females and 11 males, most of them Christian and all of them Caucasian. Nearly half of the participants had been blind from birth. The research study took two years to complete. [7]

One of the subjects in the research study – a 45-year old woman named Vicki – had been born blind: her optic nerve had been completely destroyed at birth because of excess oxygen received in an incubator. Nevertheless, Vicki appeared to be able to 'see' during her NDE.

Vicki found herself floating above her body in the emergency room of a hospital following an automobile accident. She was aware of being up near the ceiling of the room and she could see a male doctor and female nurse working on her body. At first she thought she must be dead: 'I just briefly saw this body,' she said later, 'and I knew that it was mine because I wasn't in mine.' She then went on to identify features of her clothing and personal possessions: 'I think I was wearing the plain gold band on my right finger and my father's wedding ring next to it. But my wedding ring I definitely saw... That was the one I noticed the most because it's most unusual. It has orange blossoms on the corners of it. This was the only time I could ever relate to seeing and to what light was, because I experienced it.' [8]

During her NDE, Vicki also reported visiting a very bright realm 'where everybody...was made of light'. She saw herself surrounded by trees and flowers and a vast number of people. It was here she became aware of specific people whom she had known in real life but who had since died. Two of them were blind schoolmates who had died some years before. She also encountered her grandmother who had died two years before her accident.[9]

Ring and Cooper's research provides evidence that the blind are indeed able to experience some sort of vision during their NDEs, even though their normal sight organs are not functioning. Ring and Cooper have speculated that this may involve a unique type of telepathic perception they call 'mindsight'. Their research is ongoing and may prove to be of considerable importance because mindsight clearly involves an ability to perceive in a manner beyond the currently known limits of the material brain.

Different levels of the NDE

Let us now consider the different categories within the NDE. As indicated above, a number of the experiences involve a substantially physical frame of reference. Many subjects perceive themselves to be just slightly dissociated from the physical plane of events – perhaps observing their comatose bodies, before rising into the sky above their house or perhaps observing themselves being resuscitated by a doctor in a hospital. In such instances it is not uncommon for subjects to also hear and accurately report specific conversations which have taken place at that time. At a more removed level, though – perhaps at a level that brings the subject closer to physical death – a different experiential domain reveals itself: one that the American parapsychologist D. Scott Rogo referred to as 'eschatological'.

It is here that the NDE subject may have visionary, religious or spiritual experiences – usually shaped by cultural expectations or by the person's individual belief system. The visionary material itself can be of varying degrees of profundity, ranging from a dreamlike or surreal flow of imagery through to powerful archetypal experiences. In instances like these, subjects report encounters with celestial beings, superhuman beings from classical mythology or encounters with 'God'. And sometimes they even transcend these levels of imagery, experiencing a dissolving of personal boundaries as the ego melts into other beings or forms, or seems to unite with the entire manifested universe.

Implications for an afterlife

Perhaps more than any other person, the Swiss psychiatrist Dr Kubler-Ross (1926-2004) was associated with the process of death and dying. She acknowledged cultural variations with regard to the visionary episodes different individuals might anticipate after death, but maintained that there was substantial evidence for post-mortem survival. 'For me,' Kubler-Ross once remarked, 'it is no longer a matter of belief, but rather a matter of knowing.'[10]

Kubler-Ross's medical work with dying patients predated scientific research into NDEs – it extended back some thirty years. Much of her original medical work and her earlier publications on the process of death and dying were concerned primarily with the various stages of engaging with death, including denial and self-questioning, the role of grief, and the idea of death as an integral part of human development. It is only comparatively recently that Kubler-Ross expressed her ideas on the afterlife in any detail. A small volume titled *On Life After Death*, published in 1991, brought together Kubler-Ross's principal writings on the afterlife for the first time.

Kubler-Ross maintained that her views were based on a study of more than 20,000 people who had had near-death experiences, although, unlike the Ring and Sabom studies, many of her references were anecdotal. In essence she believed that none of us dies alone, that those of our loved ones who have preceded us in death will be there to assist our transition through death, and that death, like life, is 'a birth into a different existence'.[11] Kubler-Ross claimed that she became convinced about the reality of meeting loved ones after death after researching family car accidents. In particular she was interested in the evidence from accidents where most, but not all, of the people had been killed. Seriously injured children involved in accidents of this sort were generally taken to trauma units in hospitals and Kubler-Ross was able to visit them two or three days before they died. She found that children about to experience death in these circumstances were invariably calm and serene and were always somehow assured that others would be waiting for them after death. These children had not been advised by the medical staff that their parents or siblings had died because usually there was a practice of keeping such information secret. It was thought that children in crisis would give up hope and not fight to stay alive if they knew that other members of their family had died. Nevertheless, said Kubler-Ross, 'In fifteen years I have not had a single child who did not somehow know when a family member had preceded them in death.'[12]

Many dying subjects experience a distinct separation of body and 'consciousness' – sometimes to the extent of looking down on their bodies in a hospital or at the scene of an accident – and Kubler-Ross claimed quite categorically that none of her patients who had ever had an out-of-body experience was ever again afraid to die. In her view, death simply involved discarding one's physical form in transition to a different state of conscious awareness:

Death is simply a shedding of the physical body like the butterfly shedding its cocoon. It is a transition to a higher state of consciousness where you continue to perceive, to understand, to laugh, and to be able to grow. The only thing you lose is something that you don't need anymore, your physical body. It's like putting away your winter coat when spring comes. You know that the coat is shabby and you don't want to wear it anymore. That's virtually what death is about. [13]

According to Kubler-Ross, this transitionary experience then opens out into a state of cosmic awareness:

After we pass through this visually very beautiful and individually appropriate form of transition, say the tunnel, we are approaching a source of light that many of our patients describe and that I myself experienced in the form of an incredibly beautiful and unforgettable life-changing experience. This is called cosmic consciousness. In the presence of this light, which most people in our western hemisphere call Christ or God, or love or light, we are surrounded by total and absolute unconditional love, understanding and compassion. [14]

Recent research on near-death experiences

I mentioned earlier that Kenneth Ring's *Life at Death*, published in 1980, was the first systematic overview of near-death experiences and we can certainly date the evolution of scientific, as opposed to anecdotal, approaches to NDEs from this publication. In 2009 Dr Janice Miner Holden, Dr Bruce Greyson and Debbie James released a multi-authored volume titled *The Handbook of Near-Death Experiences: Thirty Years of Investigation* (Praeger/ABC-Clio, Santa Barbara CA). Dr Holden is a Past President of the International Association for Near-Death Studies (IANDS), Dr Greyson is currently Professor of Psychiatry and Neurobehavioral Studies at the University of Virginia Medical School, and Debbie James is a Senior Instructor in Nursing Education at the Anderson Cancer Centre. The idea behind the new volume was to update key scientific findings since Ring's 1980 publication.

By and large, Ring's research has been validated by subsequent scientific studies, though not without a few modifications. There are now over 600 scholarly articles on NDEs and specific themes have emerged within the scientific research itself. *The Handbook of Near-Death Experiences* addresses such issues as the nature of pleasurable and distressing NDEs within their respective contexts, near-death experiences in children and teenagers, and claims of veridical perception in NDEs – here the researcher seeks to establish whether visual perceptions claimed by comatose NDE patients who find themselves outside or above their bodies are factually correct.

For many years it was assumed that NDEs were overwhelmingly positive in nature. Many NDE subjects reported having greater compassion towards fellow human beings as a result of their experiences and believed they had penetrated some of life's mysteries. They often had a substantially reduced fear of death, and now felt more inclined to embrace a social role that involved caring for others, even if that meant changing careers. Many also began to embrace transcendent spirituality, innately available to all, and to move away from more narrowly defined doctrinal forms of religious belief. Relatively few subjects reported entering nightmarish visionary states or having encounters with demons.

Until comparatively recently the one NDE researcher invariably cited for promoting the 'dark' side of NDEs was the American cardiologist, Dr Maurice Rawlings. In his 1978 publication *Beyond Death's Door*, published by Thomas Nelson in Nashville – a company associated with Christian fundamentalism – Rawlings drew on testimonies from his medical practice in Tennessee and emphasised the existence of hellish and terrifying NDEs. Rawlings took the view that only conversion to fundamentalist Christianity would save readers from a grim after-death fate. However, much of Rawlings' data was carelessly presented, his accounts lacked statistical data, and his text was clearly heavily biased. As a result, most respectable NDE researchers were inclined to dismiss the Rawlings publication altogether because of its lack of objectivity and extreme fundamentalist Christian proselytizing. However, it turns out that Rawlings wasn't completely wrong. In her chapter 'Distressing Western Near-Death Experiences', Nancy Evans Bush notes that a Gallup poll survey published in 1982 showed that 15 per cent of participants reported feelings of mental unrest, confusion and fear in relation to their NDEs. Some emerged feeling they had been tricked into believing in an afterlife whilst others encountered 'featureless, sometimes forbidding faces'. Perhaps more significantly, around 1 per cent in the Gallup survey had profoundly unsettling experiences, reporting 'a sense of hell or torment'. More recently, in a 1995 article, William Serdahely – a professor of health science at Montana State University – reported that four out of 12 NDE subjects he had researched described their experiences as 'frightening, scary, unpleasant', although the range of his sample was admittedly very narrow. In her chapter summary, Bush argues that because NDEs emerge via the deep psyche it is not surprising that some experiences are dark and unsettling. However she emphasizes that there is 'no evidence that these experiences are punishment for wrong beliefs of unacceptable or evil behaviour, not does evidence show that (negative) NDEs happen only to bad people.' Bush clearly distinguishes her position from that of Maurice Rawlings, whose findings continue to carry little weight in the annals of serious NDE research.

The Handbook of Near-Death Experiences also explores cross-cultural NDEs. Kenneth Ring had claimed in *Life at Death* that the 'core' NDE experience was not affected by religious belief. Although this remains broadly correct, there are exceptions. Dr Allan Kellehear provides interesting comparisons between NDEs reported in Asia (specifically China, India, Thailand and Tibet), the Pacific region (Western New Britain, Hawaii, Guam and Maori New Zealand), and hunter-gatherer regions of North and South America, Australia and Africa. Tunnel experiences were not commonly reported in India, Tibet, Guam or among hunter-gatherers in the Americas and Australia. Life reviews appeared to be absent in NDEs reported from Hawaii, Guam, Maori New Zealand and the hunter-gatherer regions. All of these regions reported NDE encounters with spiritual beings and experiences in 'other worlds' and it may be that shamanic cultural practices have influenced the way NDEs are reported. Kellehear also notes that the life review only seems to appear in cultures that emphasise an ethic of personal responsibility and conscience – such values are supported in Hindu, Buddhist and Christian cultures but are more diffuse in others. However Kellehear did find support for a universal sense of the 'mystical' and he goes out of his way to reject sceptical, atheistic and reductionist perspectives on NDEs.

One of the most significant areas of research covered in *The Handbook of Near-Death Experiences* is its summary of scientific approaches to veridical perception in out-of-body states. Establishing the factual elements in NDE perception has often proved elusive because NDEs themselves are so hard to anticipate and do not always occur in situations that are ideal for scientific evaluation. Nevertheless there is some suggestive evidence. One of the best scientifically-monitored NDE cases reported so far is the experience of Atlanta musician Pam Reynolds who had a near-fatal aneurysm embedded deep inside her brain. Reynolds was operated on by Dr Robert Spetzler at the Barrow Neurological Institute in Phoenix, Arizona, and was literally brain dead for over an hour – blood was drained from her head, her body temperature was lowered to 60 degrees, and her heartbeat and breathing stopped altogether. Although from a medical perspective her brain functions had ceased completely, during her NDE she was apparently able to observe her operation in detail from a position above her body, later describing the distinctive appearance of an unusual medical implement used during the surgical process. She was also able to recall the conversations of several members of the surgical team even though the memory circuits in her brain were not active at the time. Reynolds reported that she had had conversations with deceased relatives, one of whom forced her to return to her comatose body even though she was happy to remain in her transcendent NDE state, and she returned to waking consciousness convinced that human awareness continues after death and that 'death is an illusion'.[15]

The Reynolds case focuses our attention on the key issue of the relationship between brain and consciousness. One of the major findings of recent scientific NDE research is that it now appears more likely that the human brain should be regarded as a *transmitter* or *mediator* of consciousness rather than as the *source* of consciousness, as has so often been assumed. It may be that eventually the gathering tide of scientific NDE data will force a substantial re-examination of key issues in the familiar brain/mind debate – and that in this instance it will be the reductionists and materialists who will need to revise their perspectives.

A celebratory view of death

In May 1997 a satellite-bearing Pegasus rocket was launched above the Atlantic Ocean with a number of small containers strapped to one its booster engines. Inside the containers were the cremated remains of Dr Timothy Leary, Gene Roddenberry – creator of *Star Trek* – and twenty-two other posthumous space travellers. In what was to become the world's first space funeral, Pegasus soared into space and then jettisoned both its engines and the ashes, allowing them to fall into orbit in a blaze of light. Carol Rosin, a close personal friend of Leary's, had helped co-ordinate the mission to place his ashes into orbit. Rosin said that Leary's message to her during the last phase of his life was that all of us are 'free to ride the light' on earth and into space. It was an optimistic message, and Leary both believed it and put it into practice. His approach to death was essentially celebratory. After being told by his doctors in January 1995 that he was terminally ill with an advanced cancer in his prostate gland, Leary decided to gather his friends around him, 'to reflect on the past, help plan and design my future death, and just plain hang out and have a good time'. For Leary there could be no morbidity – he simply wanted his friends around him in a spirit of joy and friendship. 'Instead of treating the last act in your life in terms of fear, weakness and helplessness,' wrote Leary in his posthumously published book *Design for Dying*, 'think of it as a triumphant graduation.'[16]

Leary believed in the idea that you should live fully and joyously until you die. 'The house party is a wonderful way to deal with your divinity as you approach death,' said Leary, 'I can't recommend it enough…Invite people to your house party who share your celestial ambitions.' No stranger to controversy, Leary was happy to flaunt contemporary taboos around death by maintaining a running commentary about his dying process on a home website. Through to the very end of his life Leary maintained that death is a trip to higher realms of consciousness and he also emphasized that it is 'the single transcendent experience that *every* person will undergo.'[17] For him, this made the journey through death somewhat special, and something not to be feared. If we are to follow Timothy Leary's advice, this transition is something we should all plan for, and hope to do well when our time comes.

Notes

1. For well-written accounts of recent research into near-death experiences see Janice Miner Holden (et al.) *The Handbook of Near-Death Experiences: Thirty Years of Investigation*, Praeger/ABC-Clio, Santa Barbara, California 2009, Sam Parnia, *What Happens When We Die?*, Hay House, London 2008, and Pim van Lommel, *Consciousness Beyond Life: the Science of the Near-Death Experience*, HarperCollins, New York 2010.

2. Nevertheless, there are a significant number of historical cases that could also be considered as NDEs. Readers are referred to Carol Zaleski's fascinating book *Otherworld Journeys : Accounts of Near-Death Experience in Medieval and Modern Times*, Oxford University Press, New York 1987.

3   See Kenneth Ring, *Life at Death*, Coward McCann and Geoghegan, New York 1980, pp.96-97.

4   See Michael Sabom, *Recollections of Death*, Corgi Books, London 1982, pp.70-71.

5   Susan Blackmore, 'Visions of the World Beyond,' *The Australian*, 14 May 1988 (reprinted from *The New Scientist*).

6   See Michael Sabom, op cit., pp.70-71.

7   See Kenneth Ring and Sharon Cooper, *Mindsight : Near-Death and Out-of-Body Experiences in the Blind*, William James Center for Consciousness Studies / Institute of Transpersonal Studies, Palo Alto, California 1999.

8   Kenneth Ring and Sharon Cooper, 'Mindsight: How the Blind can "see" during Near-Death Experiences', *The Anomalist*, no.5, Summer 1997, p.1.

9   Ibid., p.2.

10 See Elisabeth Kubler-Ross, *On Life After Death*, Celestial Arts, Berkeley, California, p.10.

11 Ibid p.10

12 See interview with Elisabeth Kubler-Ross in Alexander Blair-Ewart (ed.), *Mindfire: Dialogues in the Other Future*, Somerville House, Toronto 1995, p.223.

13 Elisabeth Kubler-Ross, *On Life After Death*, loc cit., pp.30-31.

14 Ibid., pp.60-61.

15 For an account of the Pam Reynolds case, readers are referred to Michael Sabom's *Light and Death*, Zondervan, Grand Rapids, Michigan 1998. Reynolds and Sabom also appear in the 2002 BBC-TV documentary, 'The Day I Died', widely regarded as an authoritative and even-handed overview of near-death experiences and the mind/body relationship.

16 See Timothy Leary and R.U.Sirius, *Design for Dying*, HarperCollins, San Francisco 1997, p.99

17   Ibid., p.132

References

Blackmore, S., 'Visions of the World Beyond,' *The Australian*, 14 May 1988 (reprinted from *The New Scientist*)

Blair-Ewart, A., (ed.), interview with Elisabeth Kubler-Ross in *Mindfire: Dialogues in the Other Future*, Somerville House, Toronto 1995

Dawkins, R., *The God Delusion*, Bantam, London 2006

Fenwick, P. and E., *The Art of Dying: A Journey to Elsewhere*, Continuum, London 2008

Hitchens, C., *God is Not Great: How Religion Poisons Everything*, Warner, New York 2007

Holden, J. M. (et al.), *The Handbook of Near-Death Experiences: Thirty Years of Investigation*,

Praeger/ABC-Clio, Santa Barbara, California 2009

Kubler-Ross, E., *On Life After Death*, Celestial Arts, Berkeley, California 1991

Leary, T., and Sirius, R.U., *Design for Dying*, HarperCollins, San Francisco 1997

Moody, R., *Life After Life*, Bantam, New York 1978

Osis, K., *At the Hour of Death*, Avon, New York 1977

Parnia, S., *What Happens When We Die?*, Hay House, London 2008

Rawlings, M., *Beyond Death's Door*, Thomas Nelson, Nashville 1978

Ring, K., *Life At Death*, Coward McCann and Geoghegan, New York 1980

Ring, K., *Heading Towards Omega*, Morrow, New York 1984

Ring, K., and Cooper, S., 'Mindsight: How the Blind can "see" during Near-Death Experiences', *The Anomalist*, no.5, Summer 1997, p.1

Ring, K., and Cooper, S., *Mindsight : Near-Death and Out-of-Body Experiences in the Blind*, William

James Center for Consciousness Studies / Institute of Transpersonal Studies, Palo Alto, California 1999

Sabom, M., *Recollections of Death*, Corgi Books, London 1982

Sabom, M., *Light and Death*, Zondervan, Grand Rapids, Michigan 1998

Van Lommel, P., *Consciousness Beyond Life: the Science of the Near-Death Experience*, HarperCollins, New York 2010

Zaleski, C., *Otherworld Journeys: Accounts of Near-Death Experience in Medieval and Modern Times*, Oxford University Press, New York 1987

A Thoughtful Wake
Louis Martinie

As a Man

"Why," the woman asked.

"I don't know." I said and looked into the bottomless mysterie which surfaced in the eyes of the grieving person sitting next to me. My eyes reflected the sadness and knowledge and wisdom which peopled her steady gaze. My Mother had also just died and I could speak from commonality; from community, from deep understanding. I was at the Voodoo Spiritual Temple as a drummer and spiritual doctor. The woman's partner had just died. So many times in the past I had answered such a question with words. Now I answered with my eyes. I was privileged to share something deeper than knowing with the woman.

Death is not real until it is intimately experienced. Broad concepts of death are barren and reductive. Their generalities supply both the comforting and the disturbing answers; two sides of the same coin. They are a reservoir for the words that tear us apart again and again. As life is not real until it is experienced intimately, so death is not real until it is experienced intimately. It is best not to speak of death until one is drunk with death; until death sits on one's head and peers through one's eyes; until the mysterie is shared.

Knowledge can provide answers; at times important answers. Wisdom often takes the form of a question rather than a statement. My grandmother was a strong and knowing woman. I admired this but even more, before her death, I admired her new habit of smiling and saying, "I don't know." She seemed to be passing into mysterie. Trading surety for an open ended simplicity. Forsaking knowledge for a budding wisdom that could lightly hold both life and death.

Some questions I don't know the answers to.

If the consciousness is active and the body is dead, then is that death?

If the consciousness is dead and the body is alive, then is that death?

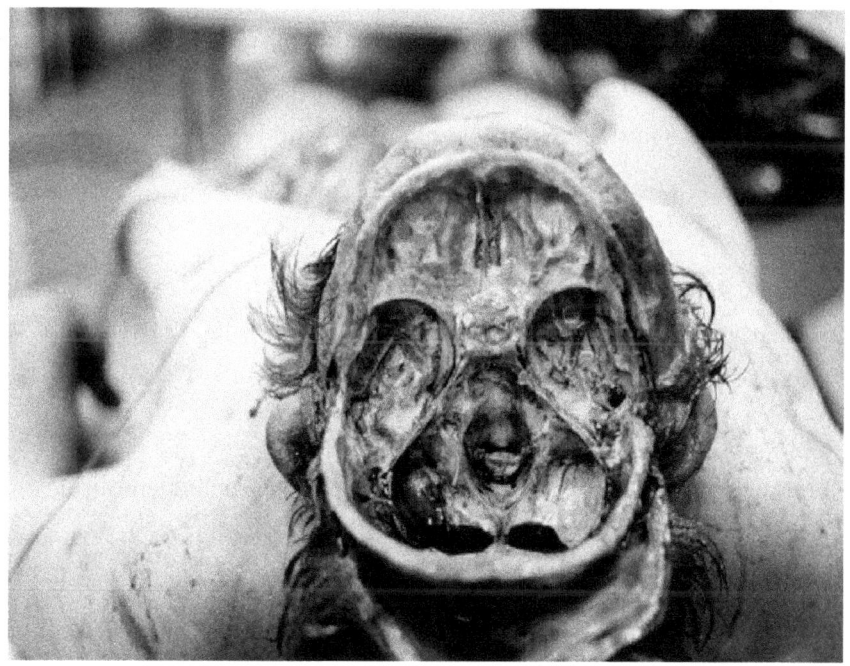

Cranium Sue Fox

Is a fallen tree trunk severed from its roots and covered with great strips of moss and flowers and colonies of insects dead?

Is a body, covered with all marvellous variety of life alive or dead?

Our bodies are colonial; they consist of many dependent and independent forms of life. How many of these forms must die before the body is dead?

As a Drummer

There is a rhythm that we are a part of and that is a part of us. It is larger than time in that it creates time. It contains stillness and movement, sound and silence. It has no name and from it all names flow. There are times, while drumming, that this rhythm finds expression in what we are playing. Fear and hope and sorrow and happiness melt into a present that is a grove that circles and spirals, and I am nowhere to be found. A lucid brilliance in the heat of the night. Beyond both life and death.

As a Spiritual Doctor

'We are composed of flesh and death, turn and return begetter of transformations.' Ifa; Oyeku Meji

Poetic transcription

The very existence of the loa is in itself a great teaching about death. The loa, as existent beings have a beginning, a middle life, and an end. There are always new loa coming into being. The stage would certainly become a bit crowded if it were not for death. The loa die. This can be a disturbing statement to voodoosants. The loa die when none remember their name. They are not called and, in time, forget their own name. This death is a type of forgetting. The ancestors and the loa share much in common. Many loa once were ancestors. Their names and deeds were remembered. They grew and passed into the state of loa.

Here is a ritual remembering the ancestors I do in the morning before taking any liquid myself.

WATERING DRY BONES

Inscribe a crossroads in the air with a cup of liquid.

Pass the cup through the crossroads in a way that it leaves your grip for a second.

During that time the liquid has passed into the invisible world.

Pour a bit of the liquid onto the earth saying,
To those whose names are remembered.
Recite the names of known ancestors.

Pour another bit of the liquid onto the earth saying,
To those whose names are forgotten, lost in the seas of time.
Allow the names of unknown ancestors to flow through your mouth.

Pour a third bit of the liquid onto the earth saying,
To those who lie within and upon this land.
Here one can honour the ancestors of teachers and spiritual friends through the recitation of the names of their known and unknown ancestors.

I finish with,

To you from the living.

and drink my first liquid of the day.

"Death is not what you think it is. That's the trick."

Priestess Miriam of the New Orleans Voodoo Spiritual Temple and I had the Mother of a mutual friend die. Priestess said to me, 'Death is not what you think it is. That's the trick.' I know that the spirits speak through her and they speak often. This single line says more about death than reams of books.

Break On Through To The Other Side
Louise Hodgson

Mind

The Tibetan and Egyptian Books of the Dead respectively give descriptions of the various states encountered after death. The stages encountered mark the soul's progression and gradual refinement as

Proletarian Necropoles Ariadne Xenou

memories and life patterns are sloughed off, rather as a snake sloughs off its skin.

These books give useful indications of the progress undergone in the 'Night Side of Life'. The Greek Eleusinian Mysteries give a foreshortened account of the life and death processes and although Demeter's search for Persephone are indicative to an extent, these Mysteries pay little heed to the progress the soul makes after death. Alchemy gives a working (and workable) model of the disintegration and gradual refinement required in the attainment of the soul's birthing within spirit but does not attempt any more than the briefest of descriptions of what happens after physical death.

I would hazard that the obverse Kabbalah; the Night Tree or the Qlipoth; reveals the soul's purgatory whilst still in the realms of Maya and thus subject to the attachments of habit and short term memory.

Purgatory, the Roman Catholic definition of the in-between experience suffered by souls who are not good enough to go to Heaven yet not bad enough to go to Hell, is the 'neither-neither' state of flux in the midst of maelstrom; a place of cleansing and emptying.

The mediaeval mind, influenced by a cruel church, is well exemplified by the paintings of Hieronymus Bosch, showing the writhing of souls in torment in a world populated by surrealistic demonic monsters. This type of hell has become a populist view of the most glaringly unsubtle kind. Hell, as the mystics know it, is a place of lies rather than physical agony. It is the realm of the misplaced, with fear obscuring fact and fallacy hiding truth.

It is time for a modern guide to help us through this momentous journey that we all have to make. A journey that is somehow familiar but that needs a good map.

Vision

Some years ago I fell ill with pneumonia and septicaemia. After days of feeling ill, with I thought, food poisoning, I was rushed by ambulance to hospital. In the ambulance I suffered a cardiac arrest. Unconscious, I arrived at the hospital and then declined into multi-organ failure, with just my liver excluded from the general internal collapse. I was in a coma, latterly drug-induced, for a few weeks.

I am mentioning this episode because of the visions I experienced whilst in this situation. I was basically dead and being kept alive artificially and was in a strange in-between state. I experienced many different scenarios – in most of which I was in some way trapped. Some scenarios suggested that I was to become a sexual plaything of a person or persons. This was unwanted by me and was never realised. At a certain stage of my coma, possibly prior to it becoming drug-induced, the visions were of a different type. I saw a lion, snarling and growling protectively. I feel this was Sekhmet. I saw arid mountains, which suggested North Africa. I saw a carved woman's head in profile, sphinx-like, with a Greek-style hair arrangement. I heard a woman's voice – "Hatshepsut is part of an ancient, ancient lineage". I then saw the deposed Shah of Persia, last holder of the Peacock Throne. At some stage a message came through – 'the War Engines are awakened'.

These particular visions are suggestive. They hint at the Yezedi, the mystical Arab tribe who lived in northern Iraq. The Shahs of Persia were part of the living worship of the Peacock Angel, the symbol of spiritual consciousness, Lucifer, Azazel, Set and more. Queen Hatshepsut, daughter of Thotmoses 1 and the only female Pharaoh, seems to have links with certain magical powers and certainly Sekhmet. The War Engines awakening signify a hugely powerful martial force being gathered together.

All in-between states suggest a half-opened door. The glimpses provided are illusionary but not without a semblance of truth.

Musings

The anonymous eternity prefaced by death; the howling, the ravages of loss, the stupor - posits a re-arranged reality that evades memory. We know but have forgotten the slow plod to immortality, the Danse Macabre, whose music is the rattling of bones and whose steps the pre-ordered temenos of time.

The Mother dies before the Child. The preface of natural order and an indicator of loss that is natural yet which apes birth as death's premature operative.

The Ancestors are a personal lineage that forms a line of trait and subtle unbalance that can only be re-dressed by forgiveness.

The mother knows that by birthing the child she exercises the round of living but the child realises that by choosing or being chosen by life, death is given a voice. "I didn't ask to be born!" is the accusation hurled unthinkingly as the cruellest of taunts. Too soon the ravages of curt dismissive estrangement cut through the carapace of filial obedience, to reveal resentment, seething and intolerable. Two-handed guilt curtails love's true expression and diseases the soul's rapture with the slime of insidious mortality.

As an ache we ask for forgiveness of sins and as innocents we cower before an idol whose name we feign not to know. How many have cowered before something unimaginable and therefore outside our line of existence? All yet none, for the dilemma is nameless.

The Sun shows up death's illusion in the clear bright light without which shadows would not exist. The moon is of itself a thing of shadows except in its fullness as an obverse sun.

Memento Mori

The Big Sleep; The Big Easy, The Big Difficult – whatever the name or phrase representing death, no one nor other can fully encapsulate this most primal of experiences. Death tends to be signified by what it leaves behind, bones, a void, or just a memory.

The above brief writings touch on facets of death but are mainly just whispered imprecations.

Death the Final Frontier
Sue Fox

I began to photograph the dead in Manchester in the early 1990s.

The morgue became a porthole to study the decomposition of the flesh, as artists did many centuries ago. The repeated shutter captured many cadavers in their expressive disjointed manners, and revealed an ever growing awareness into the enquiry of impermanence.

Through a combination of art and Buddhist practice I was using the metaphorical and literal scalpel of discriminating awareness to break

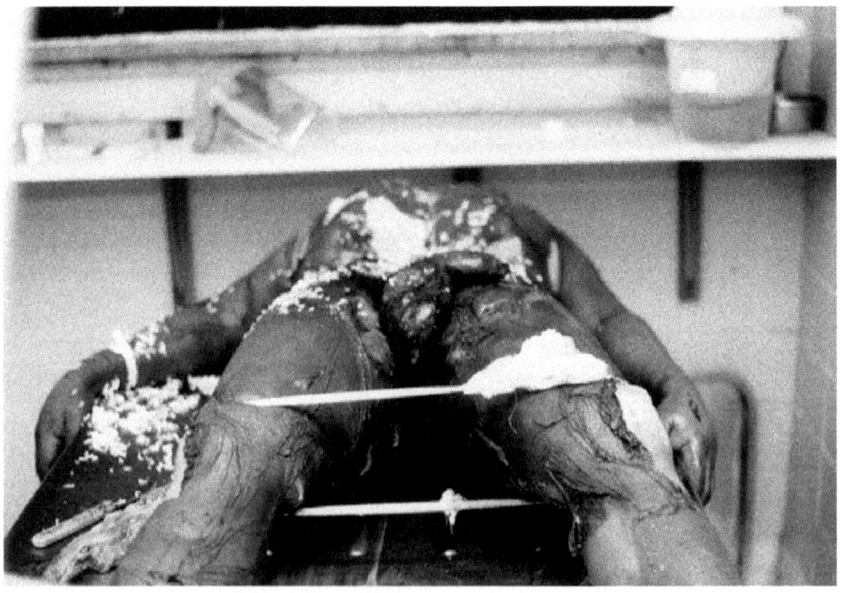

Sue Fox

down the very object which we know as the 'fixed' self. I aimed to gain knowledge into the human body but to also discard it and move beyond.

I documented the bodies of babies, old ladies, tramps, drug takers, young children and amputees for over four years.

Everybody became part of a sacred rite for me, with chanting and meditation. I felt bound to every single being through such a momentous contemplative practise. I felt the loss of life greatly. It was the loss of me and of the dead I know, and the life to be extinguished of those alive.

Death is an ever present factor

I have this forward-thinking approach of the future without me.

I captured the abject bodies in Memento Mori extraneously, the photo, the trace, the degraded image in time. A ring that said 'mum' was a poignant reminder of her status to others. A tattoo that was highly personal but cheaply orchestrated showed the sad remains of an emaciated alcoholic and his daring.

I gathered up the residue of the flesh and my eyes feasted on the terrain of skin and sinew and deeper still. The visceral soon became the lacerated and the disorganised.

I was trying to make sense of such a break down, a calamity. I was holding it in the containment of a photograph before it transmogrified any further or calcified. Now what must I learn here? What am I being shown? My eyes looked for clues. I laid my hands in the cold insides of hollowed out bodies. I felt the coldness of death run up into the warmth of my forearms and render them ice. I tasted death over and over. I gazed into glazed eyes as maggots wriggled about. I watched the house of the body deteriorate.

Is this all there is?

There is such a brutality in decay. Why is nature so bastardly? And yet there is such beauty in the wilting and the surrendering of the carcass. Disembodied we are free. Disembowelled we are empty.

The body is a painted puppet that is only here for a short time.

What the fuck will you do with it whilst you are here? Will you study it too and depict it in all its glorious form? Will you abuse and push it into extremity? Or will you nurture it into health and wakefulness? Will you record this greatness that is 'you'? The body is the most precious thing, treasure it and create and do great things with it!

The Bardo Thodol – Bon Voyage

John Power

What is Durga, that is Vishnu and that also is Siva
The wise know that they are not different from one another
The fool who thinks otherwise
Goes to the Rahrava Hell - Varaha Purana

As I get older I find myself having to read the *Tibetan Book of the Dead* more often; for friends, relatives, and even pets. One thing that bothers

Family Grave Kessarine Ariadne Xenou

me when doing this is that much of the imagery and terminology relates to Buddhism and will not be familiar to those who have not grown up within that tradition.

The Bar-do thos-grol (Anglicised as Bardol Thodol) of *Texts for Self Liberation Through Hearing, During the Intermediate Period that Follows Death* have origins back to the oral transmission of the Shamanistic tradition of Tibet called Bonpo. Those dialects would be equally alien to Westerners. The first attempts to set these principles down in writing arose in the era of unreformed Buddhism and took the form of the *Tantra of the Great Secret Union of the Sun and the Moon*, which later evolved into *The Doctrine of the Six Lights* before reaching an approximation of its present form. Essentially all of the texts deal with approaching signs of death and the dissolution of the mandala of the elements that have built the physical body, and the Realisation of the Primary Clear Light into which the elements are resolved. Obviously if awareness of these elements has been built up during a lifetime when constructing a zonule for meditation and magick, they will mean more to the post mortem consciousness of a dead person.

H.H.Dalai Lama has already addressed the problem of secularising the imagery to be expected in the after-death state in *Advice on Dying*, but as yet this has not been adapted into the secular book to be read to the deceased. Apart from the universal relevance of such a work, we can note a special relevance to the Uttara Kaula tradition of India when we realise that the Zhang-Zhung Kingdom which existed before the Eighth Century C.E. included parts of Tibet and part of Kashmir in the West. Kashmir is the Uttara Pitha; the Northern place where in legend part of Lord Siva's spouse, Shakti, came to earth in India.

This also helps to explain why the Uttara Tantrik Tradition blended so well with Tibetan thought in the *An Uttara Tradition of Highest Yoga Tantra and Dzogchen Meditation.*

The Bardo Thodol deals with three bardos or levels of consciousness experienced after death and the fourth Bardo, the Rang bzhin Bardo, is that of Samsara in the world from birth to death. This is sometimes further sub-divided into three life bardos. Once death begins, we are in the Chikai Bardo and the spiritual elements begin to build a new mandala of deities who can help grant enlightenment. Awareness of this begins three and a half days after physical death has occurred and the physical elements have ceased to function. If enlightenment does not take place or if one chooses to follow the path of reincarnation the spirit begins to build an illusory body in the Chos Nyid Bardo of the Intermediate State and this body can move freely in the realms of gods, humans, animals, hungry ghosts and demons, and future directions are decided by Karma, and level of spiritual practice. The Srid pa Bardo is the final state when the future life is decided and karmic choice of parents and physical realm are determined.

If anyone can remember past lives and bardo consciousness, it is H.H.Dalai Lama. Both he and the *Tantra of the Great Secret Union of the Sun and the Moon* go to great length to describe the signs of approaching death, other than the immediate kind brought about by physical accident, and how the elements of the body collapse; Earth into Water, as the body loses weight; Water into Fire, as urine, blood, sexual fluids and phlegm dry up and the throat becomes dry; Fire into Air, as breathing becomes difficult and the body loses heat, via the head (bad karma) or feet (good karma) first becoming cold; and Air into Ether, as the tongue becomes blue, the sense of touch is lost and breathing gives way to only the machinations of the 'internal winds', and the white (head), Clear Light can be experienced as space-like consciousness. At this time, physical death is usually considered to have occurred, but the elements continue to shut down internally. The deceased experience visions like a mirage as Earth turns to Water; of smoke as Water turns into Fire; of fireflies as Fire turns into Air; of flickering light as air turns into pure consciousness which then experiences a vivid white 'sky' symbolised by the Moon; a vivid orange 'sky' symbolised by the Sun; vivid black of a Moon, Sun and Starless 'Sky' and finally Primary Clear Light that absorbs all.

It will be noted that the first four elements shut down widdershins or anti-clockwise to the order of the mandala zonule of meditation. I personally build this with white Siva/Buddha and yellow Shakti in the East; pale blue Siva/Buddha and dark blue Shakti in the West; and green Siva/Pan/Buddha with brown Shakti in the North. White Ganesh and Dati Mata preside over the Cthonic realms of growth below. I then assume the Siva godform with the mantra 'Sivoham' and invoke 'Hrim Lalita' of the Sky realm. I feel this is the natural sequence in England. They will vary in other parts of the world, as they do slightly in the Tibetan sequence, but the Tibetan Lights can be seen as background to the deities. Not only the mandala of the Chikhai deities but also the building of the illusory body of intermediate state of the Chos nyid Bardo is formed from Sky, Sun, Moon and elements in deosil or clockwise fashion, but dissolved widdershins again before conception and finally built deosil physically in the womb. Accidental death will cause a rapid shut down of elements and direct thrust into Chikhai Bardo and is obviously not so easy to prepare for.

Given these guiding principles, it is then possible to create a book for *Self Liberation through Hearing during the Intermediate Period that Follows Death,* which is secular, or universal, rather than relevant to only one religious system. The whole process is symbolised as being 49 days between death and birth, but there is no earth time in the bardos and Karmic forces will cause time to vary.

In the Sixties, Dr Timothy Leary was quick to spot that the after death Bardos could be experienced as states of consciousness in high dose sessions of L.S.D. experience, and these could equally be guided by reading from a text which he has based on the *Bardo Thodol* and entitled *The Psychedelic Experience*. Here, the rebirth is the re-programming of the personality, rather than reincarnation. For this pioneering work, Dr. Leary deserved the Nobel Peace Prize, but instead the rest of his life became a struggle with forces of the U.S. Food and Drug Administration: Pearls before Swine!

I have tried to use as little religious terminology as possible and the ones I have used have passed into common usage since the 1960s. Mandala's are multi symmetrical patterns, to be found in various traditions, and Carl Jung adopted the format as being foremost in the symbols of the Collective Unconscious in his psychological theorising. Karma hit the top ten with John Lennon, and is the law of cause and effect in our actions. Dakinis are spirits of the air, usually female, and some traditions might be tempted to equate them with angels. I have referred to the Compassionate One as 'he' in the text, as the Tibetan version was referring to Gautama Buddha, but there is no reason why the Compassionate One can't be referred to as 'she' if the deceased practiced Goddess worship.

Yin and Yang are the Chinese names for the polarities of phenomenal existence that find the balance and resolution in the Tao. A Bodhisattva is the name that Buddhists give to someone who enters the Light but who returns to the world to help others along the path. It is my experience that this is possible while living. We can presume this is not only possible in the Bardo of life but also in the death bardos, although the Bardo Thodol presents Enlightenment and reincarnation as alternatives.

Om Mane Padme Hum:
The Jewel is in the Lotus.

The Bardo Thodol asserts that memory is nine times stronger in the after death Bardos, and that reading its text is beneficial even when alive. Even if they are not fully understood, they will be useful in the after death states. When read to the dead, it is best done by the deceased's guru, or next best by a learned person aware of the meaning of the teachings. Failing this, they can be read by anyone who reads clearly and distinctly. If the body has been buried or cremated, they are best read from a deceased's favourite chair, environ, or with favourite objects of the deceased nearby. There should also be no weeping or other distracting sounds as the Spirit is summoned for the reading. *The Tantra of the Great Secret Union of the Sun and Moon* goes into great detail as to the signs of death. If these signs are complete and, in the unlikely event, in this day and age, that the body is still present, the reading takes place close to the head. Incense and spring water should be used to encircle the body. Then the readings are made three or seven times on each of the forty-nine 'days' of the bardos. The first reading can begin once the heart has stopped and the lungs have ceased to function, but is said that the spirit is unaware of the bodily death for three and a half days and the forty-nine days are counted after this time. The forty-nine days are symbolic of seven times seven traditional planets. There is no time in the bardo. The 'days' set the course for the after death period before rebirth.

Chikhai Bardo
Call the name of the deceased

You may have heard words like these before

But may not yet recognise death

You may recognise death but not understand it

Know that if you concentrate on the words

You will perceive the Primary Clear Light

And could achieve freedom from other existences

Which form the Bardo Planes

If it is combined with good karma and earnest search for Truth

May the compassionate forces of Bardo

Know that…is passing from worldly existence

Into the next

And bring help and Enlightenment

1 As death has come

And they fall deeper into the void

Surrounded by Karmic forces

Bring strength against anxiety and fear

As the security of the worldly life fades
And they must go alone
May they be spared a long and painful Bardo
May they achieve Enlightenment

2 Enlightened Ones, Fathers of the Way and Divine Mothers
Gurus, Gods, Spirits and those who have gone before
Help to lead us along the Way
When we stray from the path of Enlightenment
Fathers of knowledge inspire and strengthen us
Divine Mothers comfort and sustain us
May we be spared a long and painful Bardo
May we achieve Enlightenment

3 May the Teacher of mirror like wisdom
Inspire and strengthen us
May his Wise Mother
Comfort and sustain us
May we be spared a long and painful Bardo
May we achieve Enlightenment

4 May the Teacher of Generosity
Inspire and strengthen us
May his All-embracing Mother
Comfort and sustain us
May we be spared a long and painful Bardo
May we achieve Enlightenment

5 May the Teacher of Meditation
Inspire and strengthen us
May his Divine Mother
Comfort and sustain us
May we be spared a long and painful Bardo
May we achieve Enlightenment

6 May the Teacher of Fearlessness
Inspire and strengthen us
May his Divine Mother
Comfort and sustain us
May we be spared a long and painful Bardo
May we achieve Enlightenment

7 May the Teacher of Universal Consciousness
Inspire and strengthen us
May his All-seeing Divine Mother
Comfort and sustain us
May we be spared a long and painful Bardo
May we achieve Enlightenment

8 May the Fathers of Clearest Perception
Inspire and strengthen us
May their Divine Mothers
Comfort and sustain us
May we be spared a long and painful Bardo
May we achieve Enlightenment

9 May the Fathers of Insightful Wisdom
Inspire and strengthen us
May their Divine Mothers
Comfort and sustain us
May we be spared a long and painful Bardo
May we achieve Enlightenment

10 May the Eastern Realm be friendly to us
Where White God and Yellow Goddess
Dwell in the Blue Sky
May the Southern Realm be friendly to us
Where the Orange God and Red Goddess
Glow in the Yellow Sky
May the Western Realm be friendly to us
Where the Blue God and Turquoise Goddess
Dwell in the Red Sun-setting Sky
May the Northern Realm be friendly to us
Where the Jade God and the Brown Goddess
Dwell in the Verdant Green surroundings
May the Central Realm be friendly to us
Where the White God and the Star encrusted Goddess
Dwell in the Light
May the elements of all the realms befriend us
That we be one of the Celestial Beings
May the Bardo sights and sounds
Be one with our sights and sounds
In the bardo may we recognise, accept and be one
With the Primal trinity of Yin, Yang and Tao

11 When the Chikhai Bardo begins avoid idleness
But be attentive to your condition
Concentrate, listen, reflect and meditate in what happens
Recognise, accept and be one with the Primordial Trinity

12 When the bardo 'dream' state comes
Avoid the useless sleep of the dead
Focus all consciousness with a clear mind
Avoid selfishness and remain alert
Recognise, accept, be one with the Truth: the Pure Light

13 When the bardo meditation state is needed
Avoid distraction
Balance, knowledge of your condition and mystic equilibrium
Recognise, accept and be one with the bardo stages
Concentrate with individual attention, free from misleading passions

14 When the Chikhai Bardo begins
Avoid selfish feelings and worldly passions
Remain steadfast, perceive Enlightenment
Be one with the mystic state of the un-born
For it is time to leave your earthly form behind

15 When the Chonyid Bardo begins, avoid fear and negative emotions
Recognise, accept and be one with what happens
Realise these are realities of the Intermediate State
It is the mid point of the Bardo planes

Do not fear good and evil forms, be detached and let them pass

16 When the Sidpa Bardo begins concentrate on your rebirth
Dedicate your thought to a positive future
The womb may be closed and you let it cause suffering
It is time for love, faith and perseverance
Avoid selfishness and meditate on the God/Goddess
Mother/Father polarities

17 If you have not realised the inevitability of death
And surrounded yourself with useless things and activities
You miss the greatest opportunity
And may enter the bardos unprepared
Know that these teachings can satisfy your needs
It is time to listen and meditate on the words

18 Listen to these words with meaning and dedication
If they are not remembered and meditated on
The Knowledge of the Great Tradition is lost
These words are most important

*

19 When destiny in life has been fulfilled
Friends and relatives will be of no help
We must wander alone in the Bardo planes
May the Gods, Goddesses, Teachers and
Deities of Feeling and Reason
Help you overcome darkness and despair

20 Alone, without friends and loved ones
Alone but for innermost mind and it's thoughts
May the Enlightened Ones pour infinite compassion
That you may have no fear or terror

21 When the five wisdoms appear
May you recognise them, accept them and be one with them
When good and evil forms appear to you
May you recognise them and accept them as
being of the Bardo plane

22 When past bad deeds cause you to suffer
May the Gods, Goddesses, Teachers and
Deities of Feeling and Reason help you
When reality thunders in your ears like a thousand storms
May it be transformed into the sounds of Truth and Enlightenment

23 When you are vulnerable and karmic forces bear upon you
May the Gods, Goddesses, Teachers and Deities of Feeling and
Reason help you

24 When it is time for you to be reborn
May dark thoughts and desires not affect you
When you are born according to your wish
May you be free from the influence of bad Karma

25 When animals roar in your ears
May you hear: OM-MANI-PADME HUM
When there are storms and darkness

May you see clearly with divine vision

26 May all who come to the Bardo planes
Seek rebirth without malice, be re-born Enlightened
When suffering and misery come to them
May they transcend pain

27 When you observe your future parents
May you see them as the Divine Mother-Father
When you are free to choose your own rebirth
May you have a body with enlightened signs and powers

28 When you have come to your new body
May you enlighten all who see or hear you
May bad karma have no influence on you
May good come to you and be multiplied

29 At the moment of next birth
May the Gods, Goddesses, Teachers and Deities of Feeling and Reason help
May you be alert in Enlightened Consciousness from birth
May you remember and not forget you previous existences

30 In all your learning, tasks and duties
May you master them effectively
Wherever you are, let all be well
May all beings you contact have happiness

31 Enlightened Ones of perfect mind and body

Of long life and great influence
Whose names, even, are sacred
Be with you and others that you may do well

32 With the compassion of the Gods, Goddesses, Teachers and Deities of
Feeling and Reason
With positive influence of the Pure Light of Truth
With deepest meditation on these teachings
May all you wish for come true

*

May your motives and intentions be pure
May all mothers everywhere achieve Enlightenment
May Enlightenment spread through the world
May these teachings be used effectively by all
May virtue and goodness grow forever

Preparation For What Is To Come
Can be read in the first 3½ days

The Chikhai Bardo
The time has come for you to enter into the Chikhai Bardo. Breathing is about to cease (or has ceased, if the reader is not present at death). You will be able to see the Primary Clear Light: a great void like a cloudless sky, or akin to being immersed in a boundless ocean. Your mind will

float freely, alone, unaided. At this time know your eternal self.
Repeat 3 or 7 times

Do not let your mind wonder. Listen carefully, for this is the time of your death. Use death as an advantage, the opportunity to achieve Enlightenment. Do this by keeping your mind clear of all negative thoughts and instead focus on the Light of Truth and the positive thought of Enlightenment. Concentrate, for it is the time of the Primary Clear Light. Meditate thus: "Even if I do not fully understand it, I accept the Chikhai Bardo. I will earnestly try to be one with it for myself and all of humanity". If death is apparent, but has not yet come, keep these teachings and inspirational spiritual experiences from earthly life in mind.
Repeat if there are still signs of life

You are facing the Primary Clear Light be alert and attentive to all that happens. You can now see and hear the Ultimate Reality. Your mind is no longer restricted to your body. It can join with the great stream of Universal Consciousness, the Unborn Perfect Enlightenment. You can be beyond birth, beyond death, free and immortal: one with the Primary Clear Light. Know that life and also death are only limited reality. Only what you experience is reality. At this time it is the Truth, the Light. As you no longer recognise yourself as mortal you can be one with the Light, the ultimate ground of reality. Recognise this, accept this, and be one with it, and you will achieve Enlightenment.
Repeat 3 or 7 times

Call the deceased by name again and say:

If you have not seen the Primary Clear Light, know that you can still achieve Enlightenment through the Clear Light of the Chonyid Bardo which follows. Meditate on your favourite Deity. Think of them as if they are with you now. Be detached from the influence of bad Karma. Concentrate and do not be distracted.

The Chonyid Bardo
The Intermediate State

In this Bardo, there will be often frightening illusions based on previous Karma. The reader must prepare the deceased for them. They can see and hear, but no earthly eyes can see the deceased. **Call them by name and say:**

Listen carefully with undivided attention. Do not be distracted. There are six bardo states: in the womb and childhood; the dream state; deep meditation in life and three stages in death: the time of death; karmic illusions of the intermediate state; and seeking rebirth. Of these, you have already passed through the gate of death and the Primary Clear Light shone all around you, and if you did not recognise it or have slipped from it, you are now in the Intermediate State of Karmic Illusions.

Listen carefully now, be attentive and alert. Death has come to you, and you have had to depart this world. While you have to face this alone, know that death comes to us all.

Do not cling to life because of sentiment or fear to go on. You have no power to stay. But there is no value in wandering as a lonely spirit. Think instead of the teachings of the Enlightened Ones who have gone before. Listen carefully so that you can be saved from fear and terror in the Intermediate State. **Meditate thus:**

When karmic allusions dawn upon me
And fear and terror can grow within me
May I realise that there are but reflections from within me
May I realise that they are a natural part of the death experience
May I recognise this moment as one of great opportunity
May I accept good and evil karmic illusions as being of my own making. Think of these words as you go into the Intermediate State. Then when illusions come you will be able to understand them. Do not forget this secret insight. When your mind separated from your body you were able to see the Primary Clear Light. It is like a mirage, subtle but bright, dazzling in its radiance. Do not be afraid for it is the same light that we all radiate. So be comfortable with it. Within the Light is also the sound of Ultimate Reality, like a thousand simultaneous thunderclaps: Om. Do not be afraid of it, for this too is the sound that we all generate. Accept it as such. The being you are now is a spirit, not a body. It is mind, not flesh and blood and bones. Know that no sights and sounds can hurt you. For now you cannot die: you are immortal. Any illusions arise from your own mind. This is part of the Intermediate State. If you cannot remember the thoughts from your previous life and from within your present mind, the source of good or terrifying visions will scare and you can wander aimlessly through this Intermediate State. So listen carefully to these teachings that will liberate you:

The 49 'days'

After the 3½ half days when the previous teachings are given, the deceased is said to realise that they are dead and on each of the following 49 Earth days a teaching is given to match the progress through the after-death bardos. Call the deceased by name at the beginning of each days reading then:

1st Day

For 3½ days you have been unaware of what is happening to you. Concentrate, be alert, so you will now recognise what happens. Realise that your existence and perception have changed. You will see sights and hear sounds unlike Earthly existence. They arise from the Mandala of the heart centre, the realm of Enlightened Realisation, where The Enlightened One abides in dazzling White Light upon the Lion Throne of the Eight-spoked Wheel embraced by his Shakti, Divine Mother of Space, radiating the Pure Blue Light of the cloudless sky. The light may shine so brightly that you can hardly bear to look at it, and bad karma could even cause you to fear it. Accept it for it can save you from a painful Bardo. The Pure Blue Light can become mixed with the dull white light of the Devas, the creators of Samsara illusion. Avoid the dull white light, as it will lead to distractions on your journey.
Meditate thus:

When wandering in ignorance
Seeking the Enlightenment of Universal Consciousness
May the Light inspire and strengthen me
May the Divine Mother comfort and sustain me
May I be spared a long and painful Bardo
May I be one with the Central Realm
Of Universal Consciousness

The 2nd Day

This is the day of the Pure White Light of the Eastern Realm of Transcendent Happiness and Mirror like Wisdom, and of the first of Six Wisdom Deities in a halo of Rainbow Light. The immutable Enlightened One of the East will come radiating Pure White Light as if from deep blue sky. He rides on an elephant throne, holds a five pronged sceptre and is embraced by the Divine Mother of Mirror like Wisdom. They are attended by male Deities of Love and Structure and female Deities of Beauty and Becoming. The White Light shines so bright you can hardly bear to look at it. It is mixed with the smoky grey-black light of Hell. Bad karma can cause you to fear the Pure Light and follow the dull light. Concentrate on the Pure White Light, accept, be one with it, for it is the Pure Light of Wisdom and it can save you from a painful Bardo. Following the dull light leads to suffering and an uncertain future.

Meditate thus:

When wandering with selfish passion
Seeking the Enlightenment of Mirror-like Wisdom
May the Pure White Light inspire and strengthen me
May the Divine Mother comfort and sustain me
May I be spared a long and painful Bardo
May I achieve Enlightenment
In the Eastern Realms of transcendent happiness
And mirror-like wisdom

The 3rd Day

It is the day of the Pure Yellow Light of the Southern Realm; the realm of The Enlightened One of the South, who will come like the Sun radiating Pure Yellow Light. Six wisdom deities will appear in a halo of light. The Enlightened One of the South will come like the sun radiating Pure Yellow Light. He rides a horse throne, holds a Jewel in his hand and is embraced by the Divine Mother of all, embracing equality glowing orange. They are attended by male Deities of Sky, Structure and Goodness, and two female Deities of Patience and Reverence. The Pure Yellow Light shines so bright you may find it difficult to look at. It is mixed with the dull bluish light of Earthly existence. Bad karma may cause you to fear the Clear Light, accept it, be one with it and the Pure Light of Wisdom can save you from a painful Bardo. Following the dull light leads to birth, ageing, sickness and death without Enlightenment, a sad interruption to your journey.

Meditate thus:

When wandering with vanity and pride
Seeking the Enlightenment of giving-feeling equality
May the Pure Yellow Light inspire to strengthen me
May the Divine Mother comfort and sustain me
May I be spared a long and painful Bardo
May I achieve Enlightenment
May I be one with the Southern Realm of giving-feeling equality

The 4th Day

It is the day of the Pure Red Light of the Western realm of Meditation, Perception and Wisdom. Six Wisdom Deities will appear in a halo of Rainbow Light.

The all-discriminating wise Enlightened One of the West will come. His body is Red Light, like the setting Sun in a Radiant Blue Sky. He is seated on a peacock throne, holds a lotus in his hand and is embraced by the Divine Mother of Knowledge and Wisdom of Radiant Blue Light. They are attended by male Deities of Mercy and Virtue and two female Deities of Song and Light. The Pure Red Light shines so brightly you can hardly bear to look at it. It is mixed with the dull red light of Earthy existence. Bad karma can cause you to fear the Pure Light and follow the dull light. Concentrate on the Pure Red Light. Accept it, be one with it, for the pure light of perceptive and discriminating wisdom can save you from a painful bardo. The dull red light leads to the world of unhappy spirits where there is no liberation and should be avoided.

Meditate thus:

When wandering selfishly and possessively
Seeking the Enlightenment of discriminating wisdom
May the Pure Red Light of the West inspire and strengthen me
May the Divine Mother comfort and sustain me
May I be spared a long and painful Bardo
May I achieve Enlightenment
May I be one with the discriminating wisdom of the Western Realm

The 5th Day

It is the day of the Pure Green Light of the Northern Realm of Will-achieving Wisdom. Six Wisdom Deities will appear in a halo of Rainbow Light. The fearless Achieving Enlightening One of the North will come. His body is green and he radiates Green Light. He rides a harpy throne, holds a four-headed equal armed cross sceptre and is embraced by the Divine Mother of Constancy and Resolution. They are attended by male Deities of Form and Clear Perception and female Deities of

Essence and Substance. The Pure Green Light will shine so brightly you can hardly bear to look at it. It is mixed with the dull green light of envy and jealousy. Bad karma may cause you to fear the Pure Green Light and follow the dull green light. Concentrate on the Pure Green Light, accept it and be one with it for it is the Light of All-achieving Wisdom. Avoid the dull green light as it leads to the world of continual conflict and chaos, a sad interruption to your journey.

Meditate thus:

When wandering with envy and jealousy
Seeking the Enlightenment of All-Achieving Wisdom
May the Pure Green Light inspire and strengthen me
May the Divine Mother comfort and sustain me
May I be spared a long and painful Bardo
May I achieve Enlightenment
May I be one with the Northern Realm of All-achieving Wisdom

The 6th Day

The Enlightened Ones have appeared to you one by one but bad karma, fear, or distraction can cause you to remain in Chonyid Bardo, unable to achieve Liberation. You could have joined the halo of Rainbow Light and achieved Enlightenment. Listen now, concentrate, be alert and attentive, for they will come again. The five divine colours, white, yellow, red, blue and green will shine on you simultaneously. Amid a halo of Rainbow Light the Enlightened Ones will come with all their attendant deities as before. Forty-two in all, including the great Father-Mother of All. They arise from the love within you. They come from the four main regions, while you at the centre make up the five realms. The deities will come in one grand assembly. The colours will shine brightly upon you. At the centre Pure Light will shine from inverted blue cups, surrounded by smaller ones radiating Pure Blue Light. From the East, the Pure White Light of Mirror-like Wisdom, like a radiant mirror, surrounded by smaller and even smaller ones that radiate Pure White Light. From the South, shines the Pure Yellow Light of all-embracing Wisdom, from inverted cups, surrounded by smaller and even smaller cups. From the West, the Pure Red Light shines from inverted blue cups, surrounded by smaller and even smaller cups. From the North, shines the Pure Green of all-achieving Wisdom, but it will not shine brightly because you have not yet achieved perfect Enlightenment. All the deities will come to you at once, the lights shining upon you. Do not move towards any of them but remain as if afloat in a great ocean of Light, perceiving all, striving to be one with all of them equally. In this way you will achieve Enlightenment. You will know that they are reflections of your own inner lights and achieve serenity of spirit. But the six dull impure lights will shine with the Pure Divine Lights; dull white, dull green, dull yellow, dull blue, dull red, and dull grey-black. Do not follow these dull lights. They lead to pain and suffering and an uncertain future. If you have not followed these teachings, you may fear the pure lights and be attracted to the dull lights. Guard against this. As the deities have come to you out of compassion, you come to them for refuge and Enlightenment.

Meditate thus:

When wondering with lust, hate, stupidity,
selfishness and jealousy
Seeking the Enlightenment of the Five Wisdoms United
May the Enlightened Ones inspire and strengthen me
May the Divine Mothers comfort and sustain me

May I be saved from impure lights from other worlds

May I be spared a long and painful Bardo
May I be one with the Five Divine Realms
Meditate in this way, recognising your own Inner
Light and be one with it,
and not slip downwards into the realms of bad Karma.

The 7th Day

On this day you will see multi-coloured lights arising from your own thoughts. At the same time, the deities of Feeling will come to you from the Mandala of the throat centre, the realm of Knowledge. Each carries symbols of death, like the scythe or blood-filled skull cups. From the mandala centre, surrounded by a halo of Rainbow Light, the Supreme Knower, Lotus Lord of Dance, comes dancing, radiating the five colours, embraced by his consort, the Red Dakini. From Mandala East comes the Earth Knower, smiling, dancing, and white in colour, embraced by the White Dakini in a yellow sky. From Mandala South comes the Life Knower, smiling, dancing, yellow in colour, embraced by the Yellow Dakini in a red sky. From Mandala West comes the Knower of the Great Symbol, smiling, dancing, and red in colour, embraced by The Red Dakini in a blue sky. From Mandala North comes the Immediate Insight Knower, half smiling, half frowning, dancing, and green in colour, embraced by the Green Dakini, also in a clear blue sky. Surrounding them, there are a multitude of deities and dakinis with trumpets and drums; banners and canopies; burning incense; dancing freely and making music that resonates thunderously everywhere. They come to reward good Karma and judge bad Karma. From the Deities of Feeling, the Pure Five-coloured Light of Wisdom shines so bright you can hardly look at it. At the same time, the dull blue light of the animal world shines forth. Bad Karma may cause you to fear the Pure Light and to follow the dull light. Avoid this, for following it leads to suffering and a long painful Bardo.

Accept the Pure Light of Wisdom. Be one with it. It is your wisdom and within it Truth resonates like a thousand thunders.
Meditate thus:

And I now fervently appeal to them for help
The Five Enlightened Ones have come to me
But I have been unable to be one with them
May the Deities of Feeling prevent me slipping downwards
May I be one with them
May the Dakinis comfort and sustain me
May I be spared a long and painful Bardo
May I enter the Paradise Realms

The 8th day

Be attentive and listen carefully. It is the day of the Masculine Enlightened One of the Mind Mandala Centre. He comes because you could not be one with the deities, which came before. He is dark brown and radiantly aflame. Between and above his eyes, he has the third eye of Transcendent Knowledge. His face is red, white and brown, adorned with skulls and symbols of the Sun and Moon. His left hand holds a sword of war and his right hand a bell of peace. His face is frightening and his voice loud and piercing. He is embraced by the Mother of Femininity. They both stand on one leg while the other is wrapped around the partner and they radiate brightly. They are borne on a platform carried by half eagles, half humans.

Fear not, they are the Enlightened Ones of the Central Realm. Know that they arrive in the form of your own thoughts. Recognise them, accept them, be one with them and you will attain Enlightenment

The 9th day

This is the day of the Thunderbolt Deity of the East. He comes because you were not one with the deities as they appeared to you before. He is white and radiantly aflame. His hands hold symbols of Conflict and Peace. He is embraced by the Divine Thunderbolt Mother, drinking blood. Fear not. Do not be confused. They are really the Enlightened Ones of the East and their forms arise from your own thoughts. Recognise them, be one with them and you will attain Enlightenment.

The 10th day

This is the day of the Jewelled Deity of the South. He comes because you could not be one with the deities as they appeared to you before. He is yellow and radiantly aflame. His hands hold symbols of Conflict and Peace. He is embraced by the Divine Jewelled Mother, drinking blood. Fear not. Do not be confused. They are really the Enlightened Ones of the South and their forms arise from your own thoughts. Recognise them, be one with them and you will attain Enlightenment.

The 11th day

This is the day of the Lotus Deity of the West. He comes because you were not one with the deities as they appeared to you before. He is dark red and radiantly aflame in a sea of blue and holds in his hands, symbols of Conflict and Peace. He is embraced by the Divine Lotus Mother, drinking blood. Fear not. They are really the Enlightened Ones of the West. Know that their forms arise from your own thoughts. Recognise them, and accept them, be one with them and you will attain Enlightenment.

The 12th day

This is the day of the Lord of the Karma of the North. He is dark green and radiantly aflame in a blue sky. He is accompanied by goddesses, some in human form and some in animal form. His hands hold symbols of conflict and peace. He is embraced by the Divine Mother of Karma, drinking blood. Fear not, do not be confused. These are really the Enlightened Ones of the North. Know that their forms are of your own mind's making. Recognise them, accept them, be one with them, merge your light with theirs and you will receive Enlightenment.

The 13th day

On this day, many fearful deities will come. First eight death goddesses come from the eight directions of the Mind Mandala. A white death goddess holds a corpse in her hand against a yellow sky, like a club, while drinking blood from the other hand. A yellow death goddess comes from the South and a red sky, with bow and arrow ready to shoot. A red death goddess comes from the West and an ocean of blue, waving the banner of a crocodile. A black death goddess comes from the north and a dark green/brown landscape, carrying a sceptre and drinking blood.

A red death goddess comes from the Southeast eating intestines. A green death goddess comes from the Southwest, with a sceptre and drinking blood. A yellow/white death goddess comes from the Northeast, also eating a corpse. A blue death goddess comes from the Northeast also eating a corpse. The eight death goddesses surround the five Deities of Reasoning which have previously come to you. Outside those, come eight animal deities: a dark brown lion from the East shaking a corpse in his mouth; a red tiger from the South, snarling, showing fangs: a black fox from the West eating entrails; a dark blue wolf from the North, tearing at a corpse. A yellow/white vulture comes from the Southeast with a half a skeletal corpse; a dark red bird from the Southwest, comes with a corpse in its beak; a black crow comes from the Northwest carrying a skull and eating heart and lungs; a dark blue owl comes from the Northeast, skull in its claws, chewing offal. Do not fear these deities. Know that their forms are created from your own mind. Recognise them for this, be one with them, and you will attain Enlightenment.

The 14th Day

On this day the doorkeepers come. The White Tiger Goddess of the East with pointed stick and drinking blood. The yellow sow goddess of the South carries a noose. The red lion goddess of the West carries a chain. The green snake goddess of the North carries a bell. They are joined by the deities and the divine mothers, death goddesses and animal deities: thirty deities in all. Do not fear them. Know that they are forms of your own thoughts. Recognise and accept them as such. Others will come.

From each of the cardinal directions six animal goddesses come. From the East comes the dark brown yak, the red/yellow snake, the green/black leopard, the blue monkey, the red bear, and the white bear. From the south comes the yellow bat, the red crocodile, the red scorpion, the white hawk, the dark green fox and the yellow black tiger. From the West comes the green/black vulture, the red horse, the white eagle, the yellow dog, the red bird and the green stag. From the North comes the blue wolf, the red goat, the black sow, the red crow, the green/black elephant and the blue snake.

In addition, the four mystic goddesses of the door will come from the East. From the East the black cuckoo; from the South the yellow goat; from the west the red lion and from the North the green/black snake. They appear many times your own size. Recognise them and accept them. Know that they arise from your own thoughts and recognise them and you will achieve Enlightenment. Enlightenment has to occur at the right time and the right time for you could be now. Flee from this and you will wander down into a long and painful bardo and an uncertain future. The Lord of Death can fill your mind with terrifying deities: glassy eyes, protruding teeth, big bellied, carrying your karmic record, shrieking "kill, kill, kill" in judgement, eating brains, drinking blood, tearing out hearts, tearing off heads. But do not be afraid.

Your existence is now only spiritual and you cannot be killed or injured in an earthly sense. The deities are not of earthly matter. Knowing this will eliminate fear.

Meditate thus:

The Deities of Reasoning have come to help me
And now I fervently appeal to them for help

I appeal also to my favourite deity and my spiritual teacher.
When I wander full of overpowering illusions
Seeking Enlightenment, may I avoid fear and confusion
May the Enlightened Ones, Deities of Feeling and Reason, inspire
and strengthen me
May the Divine Mothers comfort and sustain me
May I achieve Enlightenment
When I wander alone and
When illusions arise within me
May the Enlightened Ones with their power and compassion
Save me from fear and confusion
May the Five Pure Lights of Wisdom shine
May I recognise, accept and be one with them
When the Deities of Feeling and Reason come
When I suffer from bad Karma
May my favourite deity help me
When reality thunders like a thousand thunders
May I hear OM-MANI-PADME-HUM
When I suffer from my own bad Karma
May the Compassionate One help me
May the Primary Clear Light come to me
May the five Elements be friends to me
May I recognise, accept and be one with the five Wisdoms
May I achieve Enlightenment

Sidpa Bardo – The Bardo of Becoming – The Intermediate State
The 15th Day

If you did not become one with the Self Projection Deities of the Chonyid Bardo, you will find yourself in the Sidpa Bardo. Birth into this Bardo is unlike that on Earth. You did not know that you were dead for three and a half days, then your consciousness was reborn like a trout jumping from water.

Your Bardo body seems to resemble your physical body
With all senses and the ability to move at will
With Supernatural Karmic power
Able to see or to be seen by Bardo beings

Your Bardo body has certain forms of perfection. It is born of hopes and desires and signs of what is to come. This will include visions of the realm of your future existence. Do not be attracted to them, they lead to a long and painful Bardo. You have not been able to be one with the Deities of the Chonyid Bardo and now it is most urgent that you keep your consciousness clear of all distractions. Do this and you will be liberated without entering the womb. Meditate on your favourite deity and spiritual teacher as if they were at the crown of your head.

"With all senses and the ability to move at will" means while even if you were disabled when you were living, it will feel as if all your senses and functions have been restored and you can move freely, even more freely than on Earth. Walls, rocks and suchlike will not be a barrier to movement. This proves you are in the Sidpa Bardo. Beware of this: you are no longer restricted by a physical body.

"To see and be seen by Bardo beings" means not only that you can see Bardo beings but also those with whom you will share the next existence. You will be able to see the Gods, if you have prepared yourself with meditation. Do not dwell on these things but meditate on your guru, his teachings or the compassionate Enlightened One. You will see and hear those who are still in earthly existence. If you speak to them they cannot hear your voice or see you. If you see those mourning your loss, you can do nothing for them so do not bring them suffering. Concentrate on your favourite deity or spiritual teacher. At all times you will perceive a grey/white light. You could be up to seven weeks in this state but the effects of Karma will affect the effects of time. The wind of Karma is behind you, pushing you on. Do not fear it. Your past life has created it. There is darkness ahead and terrifying sights and sounds. These too, arise from within and your own fears. These can take the form of attacking demons, wild animals, storm and other natural disasters or angry mobs pursuing you. Flight could find you hanging over a cliff looking down white black and red canyons of selfishness, stupidity and anger. This is further proof of the Sidpa Bardo.

Meditate on the Compassionate One, master of the Primordial Trinity of Yin, Yang and Tao, and ask to be saved from suffering. If you have meditated on these things while you were alive, you will experience happy sights and sounds. You may find yourself in a neutral indifferent state, if you have not lived at the extremes of good or bad Karma. Whatever your experience, do not be attracted to it. Keep your thoughts on the Compassionate One and the Primordial Trinity. You may be restless, roaming from one temple to another. Consciousness may seem dim and hopelessness and despair affect your feelings. Strive for clear consciousness. You cannot eat but partake in terrestrial offerings. Friends cannot help you by affecting your Karmic state. It is yours alone. Happiness and suffering are your own making. Sighting of your home, family or even your own corpse may sadden you, cause you to desire an earthly body again, and set you wandering in search of such a body. Your old body is beyond use, even if you enter it. Be patient and attain the yoga state of clear consciousness.

The Judgement

Suffering is due to bad Karma, nothing more. Meditate on your favourite deity, the Primordial Trinity or your spiritual teacher. If you cannot hold to this meditation, a spirit of your earthly age at death will come and count your bad deeds with white pebbles. There are projections of your life and how you judge your past deeds. The Lord of Death will come back with the Magick Mirror that reflects your past deeds and their Karmic influence. Then the Lord of Death may appear to put a noose around your neck, drag you off and chop off your head, tear out your heart and intestines, eat your brains, drink your blood, chew your flesh and gnaw your bones. Remember you cannot die. Your mystic Bardo body can re-materialise, and the counting and dismembering begin again. Do not be afraid or try to lie to yourself. This judgement scene arises from your own thoughts and past actions. It is not made of Earthly matter and matter cannot harm you.

Be aware that you are in the final Bardo of the inter-earth consciousness. Concentrate on your favourite deity or spiritual teacher. Your state of voidness is really the radiant state of your own primordial mind.

In an instant, a great change can be effected
In an instant Enlightment can be achieved
Up to now, the beings of Bardo consciousness have come to you and if you have not been able to be one with them, this has caused suffering. But you can still attain liberation. Think of suffering in bardos as tests for your understanding. Fear not and speak the Truth to the Lord of Death.

The Importance of Realisation

Your emotions are intense and can change rapidly from joy to sorrow. Accept these moods but do not surrender to them. If your next existence is higher than your last, you will see visions of it. If you see sights that cause you anger, you will be reborn with the hell beings. Avoid anger. If you remember and desire your earthly possessions or envy those who now have them, you will be born a hungry ghost. Worldly goods are of no use now. Think of them as offerings to the Primordial Trinity. Seek yogic free-flowing consciousness. If you see religious services carried out in your name but think them done badly, you will be born among the hell beings. This is a projection of your own doubt. Meditate to strengthen the certainty of spiritual truth. When your mind is free of the body, thoughts have great strength. Meditate on your favourite deity and thus:

When wandering, alone, friendless
When my Bardo spirit body is born
May the Enlightened Ones in their compassion
Save me from fear, confusion and suffering
If I suffer because of bad Karma
May my favourite deities help me

May I hear: OM-MANI-PADME-HUM.
When the Karma comes and I am defenceless
May the Compassionate One protect me
If I am tempted to create bad Karma
May the Primary Clear Light come to me.

The Six Worlds

As you did not become one with the previous teachings, your previously earthly existence dims in your memory. Your future existence now becomes clearer and clearer. This may sadden you as you feel driven far and wide to find a new body. You will see the lights of the six worlds. The one that shines brightest is the world of your next existence. It is bright because of the power of past karma. Dull white light radiates from the world of pleasure seeking gods; dull green light shines from the world of warring giants; dull yellow light shines from the world of rational humans; dull blue light shines from the world of wild animals, where the law of the jungle prevails; dull red light shines from the world of wandering unhappy spirits and the dull grey light emanates from the all-purging hell realms. Concentrate on the brightest light and recognise it as the Compassionate One as he appears in your being. Meditate on your favourite deity and feel that they are one with you: the pure illusory form. Then meditate in the highest state you can attain through meditation. In this way, you can be one with the Primary Clear Light. After that, let your consciousness fade inward. Know that wherever there is space, there is consciousness. If you become one with that prevailing space you will attain Enlightenment.

The Process of Rebirth

As you reached this stage in the bardos and have not achieved liberation because of the teachings, but because of Karma, you feel you are ascending, descending or remaining on a level. You should try to meditate on the Enlightened One. Again, if you experience high winds, storms, pursuit of mobs, or the like, or if you have a good Karma and experience happy sights and sounds, these are only projections of your own self-made being. So will also be the signs you see of your next birthplace. As you have not recognised and been one with the previous teachings, listen carefully, for every one can understand what follows:

Preventing Entry into the Womb

Meditate on your favourite deity, as you would contemplate the moon's refection on still water: real yet unreal. If you have no favourite deity, meditate on these words. Then let the image of the deity fade inwards from the extremities. Meditate on the Primary Clear Light. This prevents entry into the womb.

First Method of Closing the Womb Door

If you have failed in the previous teaching,
the womb door will remain open.
Meditate thus:
At this time, in the midst of the Sidpa Bardo
I concentrate on one single thought
Being one with the mainstream of good Karma
I oppose bad Karma and close the womb door

And meditate on the Guru Father-Mother Deities
If you cast no reflection or shadow, you are still in Sidpa Bardo. Concentrate on the Enlightened Ones who have gone before single-mindedly. Failure to do so means a long and painful Bardo.

Second Method of Closing the Womb Door

You will see men and women in sexual union. Do not distract them as they are the Divine Father-Mother, but ask for guidance and the womb door should close. Meditate on them as your favourite deities and make mental offerings.

Third Method of Closing the Womb Door

There is birth by egg, by womb or from seeds and spores. Of these, birth by egg and womb, have much in common. Again you will see males and females in sexual union. Entering a womb now, a cave, or an egg could cause you to be born a horse, a bird, a dog or other animal. If you are to be a male, you will be attracted to the mother: if you are to be a female, you will be attracted to the father and enter his seed. You may emerge from embryo to discover you are an animal or insect and have the mental capacity and physical attributes of that creature. Or you may remain in the Bardo to wander amongst the hell beings or hungry ghosts in pain and suffering. If attraction or repulsion to one or other of the love making couples occurs, be firm and resolute and meditate. The womb door will be closed by firm meditation alone.

Fourth Method of Closing the Door

This is the method of unreal illusion. Know that the couple in sexual union and the other sights and sounds of the Bardo are unreal illusions, life dreams, mirages or reflections: they only exist in the mind. Why seek them or why be repulsed by them? If you have chosen up to now, to see the real as unreal, the illusory as true, or the intangible as tangible and continue to do so now, you may wander for ages in fear and suffering in the six worlds. Concentrate on this teaching: that all you see and hear is unreal illusion and the womb door will close.

Fifth Method of Closing the Womb Door

If the womb door remains open it is because you still believe the unreal is real! Listen and learn of the Primary Clear Light: *All sights and sounds arise from within myself. Even my mind is unborn, undying in the Light.* Allow your mind to float serenely, like pouring water into water: Turn off your mind, relax and float downstream. Do this and the four kinds of birth will close.

Choosing the womb

If you have not recognised, accepted and been one with the previous clear and powerful teachings in the heightened consciousness of the after death state, the womb door is open to you and it is time to enter within. Choose the womb carefully, according to these teachings.

You will see signs of the continent of your birth. If you are to be born on an Eastern continent, you will see a lake with swans. Do not enter there now. There is happiness and comfort but spiritual truth is weak. If you are to be born in a Southern continent, you will see impressive mansions. Enter if you can. If you are to be born in a Western continent, you will see a lake with grazing horses on the shore. Do not enter there. There is wealth and abundance but spiritual truth is weak. If you are to be born in a 'Northern' continent, you will see a lake surrounded by trees and cattle grazing on the shore. Do not enter these now. There is long life and many advantages but spiritual truth is weak. If you are to be born as a Pleasure-Seeking God, you will see temples full of gold and jewels. Enter there if you can. If you are born to be a warring giant, you will see a great forest or rings of fire revolving in opposite directions. Do not enter there. If you are to be born in the animal world, you will see caves and deep pits shrouded in mist or fog. Do not enter there. If you are to be born a hungry ghost you will see barren deserts, desolate planes, impenetrable jungles, thick forests and shallow caverns. Do not enter here. If you are to be born among the hell beings, you will hear enchanting songs carrying the force of your Karma. You will feel a strong incitement to enter, but resist it with all your strength. You will see black horses, white horses, white houses, black roads and deep pits. There you will suffer for ages the extremes of heat and cold. Do not enter there.

Escaping Karmic Torment

Behind you is the terrifying raging fire of karma, driving you on, engulfing you. Storms, blasts of rain, snow and hail, assail you. There are terrifying sounds that make you want to flee. Seeking refuge, you see mansions, caves, lush jungles and gigantic lotus blossoms. You enter a lotus and the petals close over you. There is peace and quiet. You do not want to leave. To do so means returning to the terrifying Karmic forces you fled from. You are afraid to enter a womb because it may lead you to a life of suffering, perhaps with an imperfect body. When these terrifying forces engulf you, focus your attention on the Wrathful Deity who can exorcise evil spirits. Recognise, accept and be one with one of these deities and you will have the power to choose the womb door which will benefit you. Know that these deities are born of deep meditation while in the Bardo state. Ponder the unreal illusions of your mind's creation and do not be attracted or repulsed by your own visions. But be one with free- floating yogic consciousness or meditate on your favourite deity.

Preparing for Rebirth

If Karmic forces cause you to enter a womb, follow these teachings to select a womb door. Do not enter the first womb that presents itself to you. If evil forces try to force you to enter, be one with the Wrathful Deity with the power of exorcism. You have seen the continents where you may be born. Choose wisely now: a pure realm of higher existence or impure realm of worldly woes. To attain birth in a higher realm: **Meditate thus:**

How painful now for me that I could not be one with the sacred principles of my mind. The six worlds have confused and frightened me so that I must flee from them. I act now so that I will be born of a lotus blossom, at the feet of the Enlightened One, in the Western Realm of the transcendent happiness"
Meditate thus:

Concentrate on that realm you earnestly wish to enter, using this same form of lotus meditation. Do so and you will be born at once in that realm. If birth on a higher place is not possible, or if you prefer to enter a worldly womb door, listen carefully. You have seen the continents you can be born in. Choose one where spiritual truth is strong and enter it. You will be drawn to the proper womb by its sweet smell. This means the womb is ready for entry. Whatever you see, remember it may not be what it seems, and choose carefully. **Meditate thus:**

"I want to be born the son of a yogi, or a family of high calling and virtue in pursuit of spiritual truth, so that I may be of benefit to others." Enter the womb only after you consider carefully your choice of birth, so that the womb is transformed into a holy temple. As you enter, meditate on your favourite deity or the Enlightened Ones. Do not let bad Karma fool you into thinking a good birth will come from a bad choice. Be impartial, free of bias, and what appears a bad womb, may lead to a good birth. Meditate on the Primary Trinity and choose the Middle Way. Your past loved ones cannot help you now.

If you are still in the Bardo when you hear this, listen intently to this for it is the final teaching: Concentrate with undivided attention on the Compassionate Enlightened One. Be one with him. Know yourself to be one with the White Light of the Pleasure Seeking Gods or the Yellow Light of the human world. Enter, if you can, among the temples of gold with beautiful gardens and Enlightenment can be achieved. All the Enlightened ones of past, present and future cannot transcend these teachings of the Bardos, which liberate the dead. They are now complete.

Om-Mane-Padme-Hum

You Only Live Twice

Ode bi Tola

You only live twice:
Once when you're born
And once when you look death in the face.

The above poem is found in the front of the twelfth James Bond book, *You Only Live Twice*. The poem represents James Bond's failed attempt to write a haiku, having received a reprimand from 'Tiger' Tanaka for his ignorance of the works of Basho (1644 to 1694) who is one of Japan's literary gems.
Technically the poem is not a haiku as it fails the two structural references and the seasonal reference that are the three characteristics of a haiku.

It is interesting to note that Fleming died shortly after the book was published. Perhaps he got a hint of his own mortality and that influenced his book's direction. *You Only Live Twice* is deeply racist and Fleming was a pillar of the establishment. Notwithstanding, the book is the best example of the 'Fleming sweep' as he sought to capture the richness of what was (at the time) a very different culture; bear in mind the book was published in 1964, when the idea of a single global culture seemed unreal.

The book is now part of the undergraduate coursework in several reputable British universities. *You Only Live Twice* is a bit of an oddity as it is a work of pulp fiction that deals with death and the suicidal urge as a subtext, as well as the odd relationship between two enemies. It may have influenced the relationship between Batman and the Joker, for example.

The actual poem has had an influence on me as it appears to be very profound. It seems to capture a fundamental truth that death has the ability to trigger life or heightened awareness. The mention of the 'face of death' is almost Yoruba where death is a spiritual being, said by some Babalawo's (Yoruba priests of the divination Orisha Orunmila) to be male.

The poem is not a thrill seeker's license. Bond is still recovering from the death of his beloved wife and suffering a career decline. The poem represent's someone's deepest thoughts on the great mystery. Bond is a tame government thug but he too must contemplate death, as we all must if only as a three in the morning thought. I confess that as a kid, cheerful thuggery and mayhem were very close to my heart. Death happened to other people and definitely only the old. The Who said it all when they sang,

I hope I die before I get old... now Rodger Daltrey is a sprightly man in his late 60s.

The book shows Bond's attempt to infiltrate the The Garden of Death which is owned, he realizes, by his arch enemy and the anti mother and lover Irma Bunt. The Garden of Death raises the euthanasia debate and brings it to the pulp reading community. Ernst Stavro Blofield is a connoisseur of death and collects deadly plants. One of which is the Castor bean plant which is used in some Lukumi omieros (ritual liquids).

He is also the murderer of Bond's wife in the previous book '*On Her Majesty's Secret Service*'.

The book ends with Bond suffering amnesia after destroying the castle and killing both Blofield ('the dragon within') and Bunt.

Is it the case that his amnesia reflects our inability to enter into prolonged contemplation of death which would make the ending somewhat contrived?

On Speaking with the Dead: The Cult of the Dead in Traditional Culture

Michael Clarke

Oblivion is not to be hired: The greater part must be content to be as though they had not been, to be found in the Register of God, not in the record of man. (1)

Sir Thomas Browne, Urn Burial

The idea that the dead could, upon their death, become extinguished and utterly without influence, was one that would have seemed alien to anyone who lived before the full predominance of a modern rational culture. The idea that, apart from their last will and testament, the dead could be discounted as far as the course of the future events was concerned would have seemed strange and unsettling to the men and women of the past. For it was evident to them that the dead shaped and influenced people, places and ideas long after they had departed their mortal form.

The world that tradition made was a world shaped principally by the past. Things were done in a certain way because they had been done that way in the past and worked. 'In the time of my father, or my great-grandfather, such and such had happened and such had been the outcome.' The dead remained as exemplars, their life narratives great and small pointing out the right and the wrong way to do things. Nor were they merely memories. In ancient times the barrows on the heath had been thrown up, and the church was placed on a mound on top of the site of a pagan grove. Individual identities were blurred with the passing of time but the animus of the dead still vivified the places around and about them. The land on which most traditional life was played out was marked and scored by the dead of the past. At many turnings the ancient dead still spoke with a muted voice.

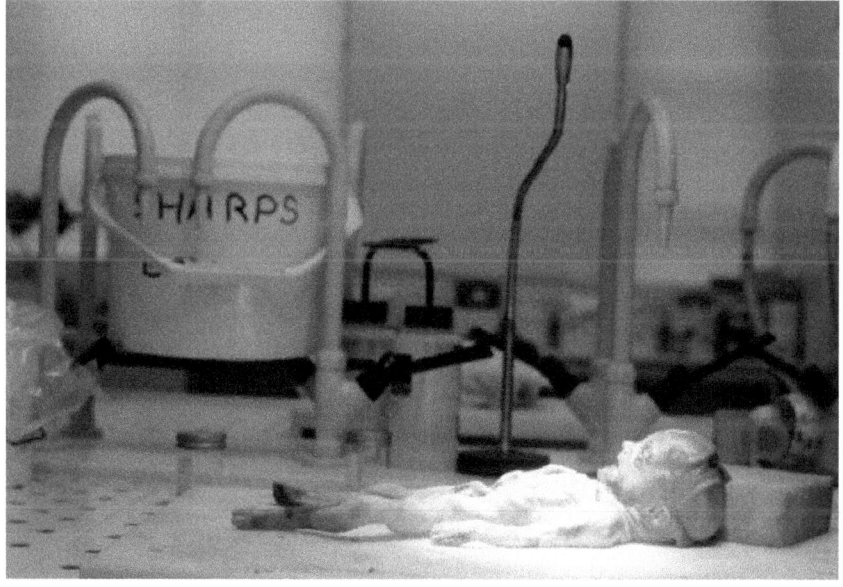

Child Sue Fox

Modern life wants little to do with the dead. The process of dying is regulated by the exigencies of clinical need. Up to a certain point the aim is to keep the living alive. Beyond that point the effort is directed at providing a peaceful passing. Once dead, the emphasis is in favour of a rapid disposal. A twenty minute slot at a crematorium, during which some clerical functionary speaks a few platitudes about the recently deceased, are all the obsequies that modern life demands. Often in the small and scattered families of today, there is little incentive to erect a memorial. A scattering of ashes ends the affair. The fading memories of a few survivors of the deceased are crowded out by others more recent and more pressing. The business of life resumes. Oblivion creeps up silently. The lives and memories of many of the modern dead terminate at a euphemistically named 'Garden of Remembrance', an adjunct to a suburban cemetery, where nameless ashes are scattered beneath a leaden sky and quiet lives lay quietly forgotten.

Yet there have always been other ways, some now considered unhealthy and morbid, by which the living related to the dead. In the folk culture which preceded and for a long time underlay modernity, the living would relate to the dead in all kinds of ways. The outcome of such relationships were beneficial in some instances and malefic in others. In the folk magic which was an integral part of the folk culture such interactions reached their fullest extent.

A key concept is that the active influence of the dead did not cease as it does now, with the closing of the hospital curtains and the journey of a wrapped corpse to the hospital mortuary. In the folk culture the nature of a person changed upon death, but his or her existence did not.

Upon death there was a clear and fast delineation of a new and different state. It was important that the dead should understand that they had died. Even those who had been weak or demented should know clearly that they were finally and absolutely dead, that they were not welcome back into their old house or could ever return to their former state. Whatever their love and affection for their former place of residence, they should know that return was forbidden to them and that their presence was not conducive to joy but rather fear.

Sometimes paintings were turned to the wall and mirrors were shrouded in the family home. The dead were no longer to pause by the mirror to look their best. There was no longer need for that. They now stood in new relation to the ancestors commemorated in the paintings on the walls. No longer should they attend to the commands of that slave driver, time. The clocks were stopped at the hour of decease and could advance no further.

The dead were, as the Bible had it 'translated' or made other, but they were not yet alien and forgotten. In some ways they were advanced in honour. A front door which was normally opened only to visiting clergy and members of the aristocracy would be the route by which the honoured but feared dead set out on the longest journey. Their transport would no longer be the accustomed shank's pony or bicycle but a horse drawn vehicle, the usual conveyance of their social superiors. The members of the funeral would be in their Sunday best or in special funeral garb, an occasion for those who had progressed in life to demonstrate some modest ostentation in their mourning. (2)

Some special rites needed attending to. The bees, that kingdom over which any countryman could rule, were solemnly told of the death lest they become offended by such omission.(3) Lest the family seem indifferent to the fate of the deceased, additional professional mourners might be hired to display in as ostentatious fashion as possible the familial grief. Such wailing women called Klagweiber attended the funeral of the writer's grandfather in a small village in Austria during the nineteen sixties. They had been brought out of retirement for one last show. Their spine chilling cries were the last cry of a traditional world itself facing its own oblivion.

The ceremonies of funeral and interment in Europe tended to be under the auspices of the dominant religion Christianity. Lessons of an improving kind were drawn. Fear of heaven and hell was inculcated. However these are hardly of the folk culture and will be passed lightly over. More important from a traditional point of view is the site and opulence of a funerary monument. In this regard the hierarchy of life tended to be reinforced with large table tombs and vaults for the large local landowner, memorial headstones for the middling sort and nothing for those buried anonymously in the Potter's Field at the expense of the parish.

It was of great importance that the dead should not return to frequent their old haunts. However, return some did in the form of ghosts. Why some returned and why some did not was to a certain extent a matter of luck; traditional thought credited dissatisfaction with the state of their earthly affairs to the majority of revenents.

First among those who returned were those who died violently. Not accepting their fate, they returned to the eye of a percipient beholder, clad in the bloody clothes in which they died. Those who died without proper burial returned to demand the rites of burial or a monument. With quivering hand, they would indicate the place of their unknown grave. Failure to observe the terms of a will might also prompt a spectre to return. Some came back through force of habit. The elderly servant associated with a place for several generations until death would be observed from time to time following his old accustomed path, in a way usually harmless and even affectionate.

The fiendish ghost was a primitive moral exemplar much feared but also much believed in. Cryptofauna of various forms, like the black dog with large flaming eyes, were part of the mental fauna of the inhabitant of the traditional world. Met on a lonely shore or a blasted heath, such avatars of Hell would prompt crossing of chests, the wearing of crosses and many other apotropaic impedimenta.

Headless horses and headless coachmen were allowed out from Hell, usually once a year, to give carriage to some local aristocratic reprobate. Early adopters of the idea that the best service is obtained by relentless shopping around for services and exerting relentless pressure on those who provide them, those pioneering free marketeers the Wicked Lords caused fear and apprehension in traditional societies. Unused to the idea that the market always works for the best, tremulous locals insisted that their pact was not with the modern world but with hell itself. Rumours of uneasy deaths or unexplained disappearances gave rise to all kinds of myths of ghostly return. The fate of a wicked lord was a lesson to all that good things must be shared and that no exceptionally good fortune lasts forever. (4)

The concern for proper and permanent burial is not a recent phenomenon. At the beginning of recorded literature in the Odyssey of Homer, Ulysses visits the Cimmerian Lands, a place of perpetual fog, rain and gloom, strange to the imagination of sun loving Greeks. There on the sea shore he encounters the ghost of one of his own sailors, Elpenor, accidentally killed, who begs the proper burial rites that his accidental death had denied him.

But thou O king remember me, unwept, unburied,
Heap up mine arms, be tomb by sea-board, and inscribed:
A man of no fortune and with a name to come.
And set up my oar that I swung mid fellows.
Ezra Pound: Canto One (5)

The ghostly dead cry out for their due from their survivors. Even today they continue to do so wherever belief in ghosts lingers on. Many and various are the messages ghosts convey, but above all they manifest by their appearance, silent or speaking, a continued existence, in despite of modern apprehensions that they are just "a handful of dust."

Only by assertive appearance may the wrong be righted and the secret revealed. It is not the mere fact that a will has been falsified, or a murder has been undetected, which exercises the spirit but the fact that they have been betrayed by those they lived amongst and trusted. That personal presence which they took for granted in life was negated suddenly and decisively. They are shocked into reappearance. They display their wounds as evidence. They point to the secret panel behind which the real will is concealed.

At the time when the rural folk culture was in its prime, death was omnipresent. Families were large. Seven or eight children were bred against the possibility that most would not survive childhood. A mother who survived pregnancy would often find herself pregnant again in a race against pestilence and death. Ten per cent of children would die in the first year alone. Another fifteen per cent would die before adulthood was reached.(6)

From cot to deathbed was but a short step. The lack of antibiotics meant that to give birth was a perilous enterprise. Death from childbed fever was all too common. The writer's great-great grandfather lost three wives, all in child-bed. He was a member of the merchant class of Bohemia, and well able to pay for medical attention for his stricken spouses. Penicillin and other antibiotics would later ameliorate this terrible toll.

In places where the water was polluted, the majority of all mortality was by infection with water-borne diseases, and the majority of those deaths occurred in infancy. The toll of the death knell was the frequent accompaniment of everyday life, the tiny coffin a frequent item of expenditure for many households.

To speak to the dead is one of humanity's oldest desires. The reasons are many. To receive the consolations of a friendly parent or relative or to retrieve some vital information now denied by the finality of death, these are the desires of the many. To a few others, spiritual adventurers, access to the dead gives absolute and incontrovertible information about the afterlife, the exact relation of spirits to humanity and most of all some notion of how to command the powers which govern the course of life and its success or failure.

The feared word of *necromancy* haunted the imagination of the common man or woman. The undisturbed repose of the dead was a particular and constant concern of humanity. To cause death is matter of grave concern, but to mutilate or in any way appropriate the inanimate dead is the stuff of horror and terrified reprobation.

To take bones from a grave or worse to disinter the recently buried is bad enough, but to take those bones and obtain personal benefits from them revolts the sensibilities of the normal citizen. Even now those killers who mutilate or dismember their victims are subject to a higher tariff of punishment. To steal bones for necromancy is to become a pariah.

Yet it is well known in folk cultures that all bones are potentially objects of great power, if by using them the spirit of the dead person whose bones they were can be coaxed to return and re animate them. In a general survey such as this there is little space to deal with the intricacies of the cult of bones.

Suffice it to say that for over a thousand years the bones of Christian Saints were accorded an immensity of respect and devotion. Held in vessels of gold, silver, glass and precious stones; adored in constant ceremony that approached to the very edge of divine worship; housed in magnificent and costly buildings; and visited by pilgrims from many different lands, the Catholic cult of saints' bones almost overwhelmed the Catholic Religion itself.

At the time of the Reformation in Northern Europe this quasi religion was destroyed over the course of less than a generation. The reliquaries were broken, the great abbeys that housed them were sold off, their buildings left ruinous and open to the sky, the fraternities that kept up their cycle of worship were forbidden.

No wonder then those secret cults of bones survived, the reported Ancient Order of Bonesmen of East Anglia being but one example. Bereft of significance by the dominant culture, the cult of bones became the preserve of the professional bonesman, an artisan of bone work, who nonetheless claimed amongst those who believed in him powers equal to and exceeding those of the former priestly custodians of bones.(7)

Sometimes it is not enough for a mere spectre to appear. The very dead themselves are roused to life and cast aside the coffin lid and tomb to appear in the flesh in the form of a ghoul or vampire. The dead who most refuse to go away fasten on the flesh and spirit of the living and drain them of their life and health.

Whole encyclopaedias are now devoted to the minutest doings of the vampire, who has become emblematic of the evil dead in modern culture. As belief in the survival of the spirit has waned, belief in the vampire has advanced. Vampires, in their original milieu, tended to be characteristic of Central and Eastern Europe. As modernity progressed vampires were adopted into the cultures of Britain and the Americas with gusto. Now they are so much a part of mainstream consciousness, their name, nature and the methods needed to defeat them are common knowledge in a way characteristic of few other folk devils.

Vampires are part of the folk culture and mass popular culture simultaneously. It may be useful to speculate why this species of living dead are so popular. In their original setting, the peasant societies of Central and Southern Europe, it is hard to escape the impression that Vampires represent in some way the burden of life lived under an inefficient and oppressive government bureaucracy, whether those of the Hapsburgs or of the Turks. The life was sucked out of the peasant by extortionate taxes and rents. He or she was becoming aware that the quasi divinity of the aristocracy and established church were screens for a vast bureaucracy leeching out his sustenance.

Transposed to societies guided by principles of modernity, the representations of the vampire seem to be transposed. The vampire becomes more erotic and the act of blood sucking becomes a semi sexual act. The aristocracy of the vampire is enacted in already ruinous castles. That power is in the past and its actual power over countless lives is diminished.

The strength of the contemporary vampire is enacted principally through sexuality. With an ability to disrupt the best planned of careers and the nuclear family typical of this phase of society, the vampire became the vamp, an early derogatory title for women who expressed their sexual preferences and lived their life according to their desires.

In more recent years the popular vampire novels of Anne Rice (8) and Poppy Z Brite (9) testify to a further sexualisation of the vampire motif. The gorging on blood of the vampire becomes in the novels of Rice something like the taking of a mind altering drug to her young but fragile vampires. In the novels of Brite another key twentieth-century motif comes to the fore, the serial killer, who is mixed together with vampire lore in a potent cocktail of blood and fear.

Another method, by which the dead were supposed to return, particularly in the first half of the twentieth century, was by way of spiritualism.

Direct contact between the spirits of the dead and a living human being had been exceptional and extraordinary before the mid nineteenth century. Although accounts of spirit evocations stretch back to antiquity they tended to occur between individuals of an exceptional cast of mind and of irregular beliefs. They were the province of the ritual magician or the cunning man.

The great mechanised wars of the twentieth century led to the loss of life of millions of combatants on a scale unprecedented in world history. The shock of the losses to many of those that survived led to an equally unprecedented upsurge in the practice of Spiritualism and the establishment of Spiritualist churches of many different kinds.

What was needed was a way that one of the bereaved could contact the spirits of the dead without seeming to be part of any occult culture. Spiritualist churches allowed for a form of spirit contact to be achieved whilst at the same time maintaining a proper air of respectability. The atmosphere of the church with its prayers and hymns induced an air of seemly devotion to the proceedings.

Even when the immense trauma of machine-war waned and was forgotten, the apparatus of spiritualism managed to keep itself intact. In new settings, like the conference suites of a suburban hotel, new mediums of a therapeutic kind kept the appeal of spiritualism alive. What is on offer now is a kind of spirituality with not only the occultism left out, but with most traces of original tradition or non-modernity left out as well.

The returning dead, who appear in spiritualist séances, now tend to be guides to life, moral exemplars in a world in which the traditional Christian sense of sin seems to be rapidly dissolving. These spirit guides cross continents and forswear their own cultures in order to attend a meeting room somewhere in suburbia filled with women of a certain age in search of moral certainty. Typically a spirit guide will be an American Indian. His moral profundities will extemporise on the need to save the planet, to be kind to those of other races and different social circumstances and above all not to give up hope.

If there is one message that the dead bring from the time of Homer onwards it is that life is so precious that all of it must be enjoyed to the full, for as much of the time as possible. An air of resentment surrounded the departed. With so many good things on offer in the world why had their death denied them even a small portion of such munificence?

The condition of the dead is, they tell us, one of cold, hunger, neglect and above all powerlessness. If only they could return and make a few simple changes, so many undesirable consequences might be avoided. Even great heroes would rather serve as a slave in the house of a swineherd if such servitude could bring them back to life.

So they take steps to return, not all of them desirable to their survivors. It is no surprise that the great Psychopompos and the Guide of Souls of the ancient world, Hermes, is also the god of the fourfold phallic Herm. The wand of Hermes which he uses to usher the twittering bat-like souls of the deceased to Hades is also the phallus which will return refreshed souls to the Land of the Living. (10)

The spirits of the dead in Homer's Odyssey, push and jostle to be near the L shaped trench full of bull's blood, which they hope will reinvigorate them.(5) The living dead crave blood as their passport to even a shadowed life in the land of the living. The incubus and succubus couple at will even with the ugliest and oldest, just so that they may have the chance to convey their demonic progeny back to live the life of the living.

The vigour of the belief in the continued power of the dead was both a disability and a consolation for dwellers in traditional society, The peasant cringing in his cottage for fear of Vampires, cloves of garlic hung around his neck, could be said to be disabled by his belief. The believer in the cult of Saints' Bones might even now be said to be wasting their time in superstitious expenditures and unnecessary travel and needless donations. And yet what a great quantity of fine music, works of art, architecture and literature was inspired by belief in the continued power of the dead.

It is fair to say that the quality of bleakness and terminal tragedy sometimes inspired by modern illness, death and funeral rites was probably only present in the past for the very poor and outlaws who were outside of the embrace of traditional society.

By making of death a continuity rather than an absolute decease, traditional society allows the residual potency of the dead to be reflected back upon the living. In tribal societies such as those of Central Africa specific roles are assigned to the dead and living. It is a tragedy for both if the ancestors are forgotten. The wisdom of the ancestor augments the power, the Muntu, of the living. (11)

No such concerns inform the role of ancestry in modern life. They are dead and gone. That is all there is to say on the matter. Any other belief may seem laughable to the inhabitant of a modern city. It is hidden away from the common gaze in its seeming old fashioned self indulgence.

Part of the price we pay for a belief in only the rational and provable in the conduct of life is a paucity of expression and a diminution of consolation. Some may take this choice cheerfully but others may rebel against the frame of mind that produces it. In modern Britain in particular death has replaced sex as the great unmentionable. For two generations it has been relegated to a far distant corner of the mind, present but quiescent, a reproach to the life lived for secular objectives, but something difficult to deal with, uncanny, but occasionally insistent.

It is welcome that here and there the talk is beginning again. The consequences of reinstating the dead to their former centrality could be as great as the sexual changes that revolutionised the society of the Twentieth Century. Just how such a process would work is difficult to speculate about at present for it relies on deep changes to the idea of modernity which will inevitably emerge as the century progresses.

And therefore it cannot be long before we lie down in darkness, and have our light in ashes: (SIR THOMAS BROWNE; Urn Burial.) (1) To *have our light in ashes*, to make the dead central again rather than marginal might seem like an absurd dream of a demented traditionalist. However, the deep dreams of a culture can develop in ways quite un-thought-of by those who guide social and political policy by rational means.

Now that the great engine of the imagination rather than the great engine of fear tends to guide the conduct of individual lives, now that the imagined world is the ultimate good, this deep force of the imagination may produce new and undreamed of illuminations of mortuary thought. Just as the first secret world of Hermes the Erotic dominated the imagination of the Twentieth Century, so the Twenty-first may be motivated by his other secret world, that of the Way to Hades and Oblivion. (10)

References

1. BROWNE, Sir Thomas 1956. The Religio Medici and Other Writings. J. M. Dents and Sons Ltd. P. 135

2. THOMPSON C.J.S. 1932. The Hand of Destiny, Everyday Folklore and Superstition. Rider and Company. Pages 174-192

3. JOHN GLYDE JUN. Ed MICHAEL WATKINS. 1973. Folklore and Customs of Norfolk. EJP Publishing Ltd

4. WESTWOOD J AND SIMPSON J. The Penguin Book of Ghosts. Introduction. Introduces the main ghost types. The text contains examples of the different types.

5. POUND, EZRA. The Cantos. A Draft of 30 Cantos. Canto I P.8. Faber and Faber 1955.

6. SHARPE J.A. 2007. Early Modern England, A social History 1550-1760 Chapter 1 Population. Hodder Arnold

7. PENNICK N. 1995 Secrets of East Anglian Magic. P. 62 The Bone Magicians. Robert Hale London

8. RICE. A.1991. Interview with a Vampire. Time Warner Paperbacks

9. BRITE P. Z. 1994. Lost Souls. Penguin.

10. KERENYI. 1996. Hermes, Guide of Souls, Spring Publications U.S.

11. TEMPELS, PLACIDE. 1969 Bantu Philosophy. Presence Africaine.

Body

Mishlen Linden

What, then, can we say about death? Each religion has its own stories, but they are all in agreement on the idea of the immortal soul. I can only speak about events that have touched my life. I can only believe what I've seen, felt, and heard. Death, divorced from dogma.

My first encounter with death came when I was about 8. In those days, a laundryman would pick up your dirty clothes and bring them back clean.

One day, whilst I was in the car with my mother, we found him after an accident. There was a lot of blood. He had been thrown from his little truck. We were shocked. The ambulance came and took him away. When we went home, I went to my aquarium filled with fish, and prayed that God would take the lives of these fish in return for saving my laundryman's life. Well, the fish, one by one, died and he recovered. Whether that was my first spell, I don't know, but I did perform it.

This is a typical encounter with the scapegoat practice. Killing one, that another may live. I didn't kill the fish, but I was exchanging life for life. When the sacrifice is not your own, it is a questionable morality that gives you the right to take another's life.

Death; human death. It seems that when it comes, whatever one faces, one does so with their own beliefs which reflects their understanding and their experience. In reality, it may be much more abstract. We add the details.

Death is inexorably twined in life. To think about death, one must think about life. One is bound to the other. Pro-choice versus pro-choice. I have had abortions, and I have miscarried. Each was different. I want to compare them; the entrance to, and this early exit from life. Because each was different, and the woman so burdened should make her own choice, for only she would know.

To start at the beginning; conception. My first encounter with pregnancy seemed to me a mistake. There was a developing physical body forming inside me, yet I felt no life within it. In the end, I miscarried. I had felt no soul within me, and being young, was rather relieved.

The second time, I still felt no soul within me. In a room filled with other women, waiting for an abortion, I took a survey from them and found that no one felt sentient life within them. This led to my belief that no soul had yet incarnated. In fact, when I talked to various women in different stages of pregnancy, it seemed that the soul's incarnation could appear at any time during pregnancy and even at 'birth'.

Some felt it immediately, some felt a soul months later, and some not until birth.

My final personal experience with incarnation was quite different from earlier ones. During my lovemaking, I saw a bright ball of light descend and rest in my womb. Oh-oh, I thought. In the morning it not only was still there, my breasts were sore and swollen. And, oh, I felt a soul. I was in the stages of getting divorced and had no ability to do this by myself, and so I had another abortion. I talked to the child, explaining that this could not be. I felt an acceptance from it. I gave him up, and within a week, my lover's wife became pregnant, they had the child, and it looked just like me! A more willing womb had been found. He sent me a picture...we both knew.

I concluded that each choice in pregnancy could only be decided upon by the woman, and it seemed from my questions that most abortions did not include the soul-and such a thing could only be known by the host-mother, and that the choice remains hers. So much for conception.

At the other end of the spectrum lies death. Death seems to be the proverbial onion skin, and how many bodies do we contain? What stays and what goes? Religions seem to be based around how one dies, and what happens afterwards. And so they fight on; dogma after dogma. Some forms of Christianity believe in only one life, and the judgement is cast upon you into the swarming seas of eternal heaven or hell.

It is my experiences that teach me, rather than a shared belief system, and my experiences have been quite complicated. When that which is living departs from that which is dead quite a lot of baggage goes with it, it seems. I am old enough to have seen friends and family die around me.

I will relate here some of my experiences: The Egyptians split our selves into the Ka and the Ba. Others say that there are more than two bodies, and I must agree for I have met them. When a person you are close to or have been close to dies, your internal relationship with them comes to the fore. While they are undergoing their own process of change, bits of their personality, their talents, even likes and dislikes are flung off just as the body has been. These characteristics come to rest within the most congruent, closest sources. This would generally be from ones lover, family or close friends. So the circle expands. Therefore, NOTHING is lost to us, as a racial consciousness. At some point, these characteristics become part of them, of us.

Mr. Norbu (Taxter Rinpoche, an elder brother of the Dali Lama) once told me that one of the most important things for us to cultivate within ourselves were established good habits. He said that if you don't establish them while living, how will you act when you die without them? These good habits may help you in getting through the bardos or purgatory or wherever your beliefs lie, but also, they are like a great present from your friend, and they become a part of you.

Some years back, Lu (my companion) and I were staying in Bloomington, Indiana for the summer. One night we each had a separate dream about shovelling dirt into a grave. Upon rising, the smell of roses was strong in the air. Later that day, we learned of her death, a stroke while in ritual. No one could tell if it was a trance possession or a physical illness-and it was too late when they found her. Her name was Rose, and we realized that the dream was her way of talking to us, saying goodbye, she was gone.

Such things are not uncommon. Quite ordinary people have them, but rarely speak of them. When my father died suddenly, his astral body made the rounds of the couples my parents had tended to hang out with, saying his goodbyes. The only person, actually, who did not see him, was my mother. Perhaps she did and denied its reality as although she was the psychic one she was afraid of seeing things. When dad came to me, I did suggest that he leave her because it would only freak her out (I was young in those days, and rather stupid). So perhaps she did; but being an atheist, denied visions with a staunch belief that there is no tomorrow. I learned to keep my visions to myself at a very young age.

When she died, she died slowly from cancer, and in a lot of pain. The day before she died, I had been with her. The doctor predicted that she would live another 6 months - something she dreaded. I had given her a gau (a Tibetan locket) with some of the Medicine Buddha sand in it, so that she would pass more quickly. I then went home to New Orleans to wrap up affairs before joining her. The night soon after arriving home, we got a call that she was dying, right then! A plane would have been too slow, so we broke speed limits in 4 states. While Lu drove, I focused on her and her state. It was 10:30 when I saw her leave her body, terrified, screaming. She fairly tore her way out, up and above; but then something unexpected happened. Her flight curved and she came back down, somewhere in eastern Kentucky; an immediate re-birth! I took note of the time, and when we reached the hospice, I was not too surprised to learn she had died precisely then. Yet, when I sold her house, I felt her behind me, and she was gloating over the money. What part of her had stayed earth-bound?

Death is a complicated issue

A friend of mine, a brilliant artist and self-destructive magickian, died a few years back. Recently I have been feeling him about. Talking to a friend, he also has been feeling him. I was working on a large Icon (I make religious sculpture - god and goddess and the little spirits of the world) when I took a look and found that the face I had been working on had turned itself into the goddess-face my friend had been used to carving into wood and skin. Yes, he was there.

A man I had worked circles with died, in an accidental smothering during an epileptic fit one night. I would have thought he would have known what to do. I went into his spirit to see how he was. He had always been known for verbosity, and that had not changed. He was terrified, in a dark place, with eyes all around him, glowing. He had found if he did not stop talking to them, they could go no closer. And so he talked on and on...to him, he was holding death at bay.

Another type of death is found in lineage. Once you have found your teacher, you are never left alone, especially once he dies. My own Teacher, still alive, is often attended by HIS teacher when he is giving teachings. Part of the teacher, by choice, will stay after death and influence his student, continuing his education... Mine used to say that after his had died, he saw him far more often. I could see this man, standing behind him, speaking as my teacher did. I know this is true. (as well as listening to them both at the same time! :) For those with sufficient power and awareness, one may choose how far one wills to go, but this is known only by the very wise. One can logically conclude that his teacher's knowledge is built from his own teacher, who learned from his teacher, and on down through the ages, when the lineage began.

Moreover, that teacher is in contact with all the teachers down the line of years, the accumulated wisdom of the ages. Imagine that! That is what you accept when you attract a teacher, his lineage, lifetimes of experience. This is not always done by word of mouth but rather by mental connection. A lineage can be most important! And, ultimately, you become the teacher and carry it on. Consider the responsibility of this, you become the Sacred Vessel. And consider what part of the Self does this, if the soul moves on? There are many, many layers!

I have concluded that each person's death brings an experience that is unique to them. When Mr. Norbu died, we all grieved; as did many around the world; even though it would bring him a new life; inside the walls of Tibet; as he wanted. I had always thought I'd be with him when he died. So did Sandy, a fellow sangha member. She had spoken to him shortly before he died and he had told her 'you will all be with me when I die'. I had thought the same, but on Malkuth, it wasn't so. In my grief, as I looked at his body, it was empty. I had thought some part of him would linger there awhile, and here he was, dressed in the robes of state, holding bell and dorje on his throne, the Dropung monks chanting for him as we prostrated before him. But I couldn't find him! He had told me, years ago, that the last thing he wanted to do before he died was to circumambulate our Enlightenment Stupa. I walked out then. I felt driven to it. My feet pounded into the ground as I walked. However, when I reached it, instead of walking around it, I went up and climbed what I could and hugged it. I mourned him, missed him. And then I clearly heard the words 'I WILL be back'. I let go of the stupa. I felt better, although I knew I'd never see him again in this body. I let go of the stupa (before someone saw me!). I had been able to reach him, be with him, all within 24 hours of his body's death.

Some days between day 1 and day 40 after his death, Lu and I once again had a 'shared dream'. I was simply an invisible watching spirit. I was watching the birth of two babies - twins, in Tibet. Lu was closer; he was seeing this with the eyes of the midwife. One was Mr. Norbu. The other was a monk who had been following him through his lifetimes, a guardian, some thought. I excitedly drove to the monastery to tell everyone-but they already knew, of course.

Some parts of the dead watch the living, and yet some part of your personal atman, or soul, goes on into its next incarnation. So it comes down to this question - how many bodies do we have? I cannot give you an answer-yet-but I am tracking the desire bodies of the soul. Eventually, we will All Know, and then Forget again

I think there is no single answer. Death is when our final aggregates of source and form come together to shape our destiny. I expect we have many, many bodies....here, and elsewhere.

The Great Western Hoax
Odi bi Tola

Yes, I live in the West but I do not buy into The Hoax. The Hoax is a product of the imperialistic wars and battles for ascendency that our nations have indulged in for over 300 years. The Hoax has now proven to be an integral part of the Neo - Colonial mindset that still permeates the black world. I live in the West but am not fully Western. A part of me hearkens back to forms of suppressed wisdom from a previous era. Christianity has become a totalitarian religion. Even despots and corrupt dictators now spout the anti pagan creed which stemmed from Christian doctrine. The worst thing about this suppression is how internalised and universal it has become. Those who are the biological inheritors of the suppressed indigenous pagan view now eagerly continue the suppression of the slightest hint of this indestructible wisdom. I believe that we are entering new dark ages- an age of a dark materialistic soul. This wisdom is indestructible because it may lie dormant for a generation or two before spontaneously reappearing in a younger generation. This knowledge comprises the social management of death (i.e. how to have a good funeral) but also the inner acceptance and new developing relationship with those that have died, as their essence is still with us.

I have a right to be critical, as that is the only way that I can improve the West or just gain concessions for those who wish to experience separate sensibilities to the prevailing ones. I have a moral right to be critical, as people are still dying and funerary rites are not being performed properly which then goes on to an unstructured mourning and further needless misery generated for many sensitive people who do (or should that be 'cannot') believe that this is the end.

The proper rituals and observance of death are not to be found in ritual chasing actions but are far simpler. Death requires that the living gather in a wide community and also that the individual mourners observe some kind of inner activity and remember the dead in sensible prayers (from the heart). The dead are close by at all times to aid and gain sustenance from us.

A recent painful example of the prevailing mindset will illustrate the personal and private tragedy that arises when The Hoax is believed.

A woman of great intellect recently lost her eldest son in a motorcycle accident. The young man's corpse lay in a field near the road where the accident occurred, for over twelve hours. The young man died alone. Given the horrible nature of the child passing before the parent the situation was further compounded for his mother who explained that, 'he had died alone in a field'.

She had called me out of the blue and, crying, narrated the facts. I was surprised and immediately went into my priest mode and started making suggestions. I was working from the heart. She immediately cut me short stating that she did not believe in such things. I tried to explain that what I suggested was not specifically occult or esoteric but could equally be viewed as psychological role play that would give her some comfort; but she would not have it. I wanted her to suspend her disbelief in order to allow a different reality to emerge from within. This suspension of disbelief is the basis of most psychotherapeutic modalities and also entertainment.

What was clear was that she was stuck in grieving without a structured coping mechanism. She made an attempt to go to a bereavement counsellor but this did not relieve her situation, as she could not enter into the therapeutic relationship with the counsellor which was a prerequisite which would have increased the likelihood of her recovering more quickly. It was also interesting to note that the community grief process that her friends and well wishers offered seemed to have a finite period after which they acted like she should have got over her loss. She was left to have a funeral with just her nuclear family, as opposed to the more fulfilling way it is done in the Caribbean. I do not consider this to be a civilised mode of conduct.

I would not have minded if said prevailing sensibilities had some sort of empirical or experiential basis. As usual, the prevailing view is formed by the wholesale pronouncements of the unintelligent popular media and individual 'talking heads' of the humanist/atheistic persuasion.

I would argue that The Hoax is the prevailing view that death is an almost secular and decidedly physical affair whereby a biological machine ceases to function and that is that. It is not what is said that should be examined but how people choose to act.

Even when authors like Jean Kerboull have written about Haitian Voodoo (*Voodoo and Magic Practices*, 1978) in a generally sympathetic manner they have further propagated The Hoax when they consider the role of grave dust in malefic magic. They attribute the harm done to victims to a primitive form of biological warfare and cite the proximity of cholera and other pathogenic bacteria in explanation for the illness seem in the victims. Sadly many curious people are so desperate for new books on Voodoo that they end up being pathetically grateful for books that subtly misinterpret or misrepresent core concepts such as the use of grave dust.

The clinical symptoms of cholera are singularly distinctive and cannot be mistaken for anything else and these authors seem to ignore the fact that a number of gravediggers get into intimate contact with grave soil on a regular basis and do not succumb to diseases like cholera. Not only that but anyone that has lived in the Caribbean is likely to have seen cattle, goats, sheep and chickens grazing or pecking amongst the graves without harm to themselves or to those further up the food chain. Cholera is a notifiable disease in the West Indies and most of Central and South America.

This article looks at my direct experience of funerals and death in the Caribbean during the period of c1969 to the mid 1990s.

All-yu bear wid mi (translation: You chaps bear with me).

Yu will understan' where dis story going laitah (You will see where this narrative is going letter on).

Leh we goh (let us depart)!

My Sunday mornings by 1969 represented the height of aspirational eating in our Guyanese/British family. We would invariably have one of our Sunday morning treats like tuna. No; it wasn't tuna loin, which was more 1990s than 1960s. We were proud to have canned John West Tuna. As Guyanese (except for my weedy kid brother who was born in England) we were happy to have fish for breakfast. We also had orange juice - Birdseye Florida Orange Juice was a frozen concentrate that had to be diluted with water. Mum and Dad also had freshly percolated coffee from a Cona Coffee Percolator. I found the whole ritual of coffee percolation fascinating and the smell was wonderful; I just did not like the taste at the time. Later on that Sunday, we were going to have one of my mother's first Italian dishes as a side dish, - macaroni cheese! Macaroni cheese then went on to conquer the Caribbean but some called it macaroni pie, as they do in Barbados, and it was a social signifier that indicated travel to the 'mother country', and aspirations of greater sophistication by embracing foreign cuisine.

One Sunday morning at breakfast, Dad announced that he wanted us to discuss where we were going to live. Dad was, in his own way, quite a progressive parent at times. He had recently graduated from Vauxhall College in London with an HND in Building Construction and was willing to move on to somewhere else in the world to get away from the UK winter and the negative prevailing social attitudes to the 'darker races'.

We had a choice go to Australia or go back home? Our choice was unanimous – Guyana! The land of my birth and the country that had morphed from my parent's B.G (British Guyana) to Guyana, in the 1960s when it achieved independence from the British upon independence but was still home to my parents (at least in those days).

As kids we truly imbibed 'For Queen and Country' from our patriotic parents and we were happy to be a part of the Commonwealth.

My parents were at pains to prepare me for Guyana and were very concerned that my great love of reptiles and insects would lead me to get bitten by the numerous indigenous poisonous animals if I continued my schoolboy naturalist habit of turning over stones to see what lived under them. My mother was also quite concerned that I did not bring anything into the house as I earned myself a *fine cut tail* (beating) from bringing sloe worms (a species of British legless lizard) into the house a few weeks before the momentous decision to relocate, thus giving her a nasty fright as they so resembled snakes.

Guyana

When I was born in British Guyana, my maternal grandmother noticed that I had a small depression resembling an ear piercing on my left ear. My brother also has a similar mark on his ear. The mark has moved, as ears grow throughout life.

My Grandmother took this mark as a sign that I was a 'returner' as she held me one day as a baby. She went on to claim that I was the reincarnation of a deceased Churchwarden of her acquaintance that had lived in the next village. I am told that I gave a little start and shot her a stare when she first made that comment and she nearly dropped me, much to my mother's consternation.

My family are visibly black but like most Guyanese are actually a bunch of mongrels. The following nationalities have contributed to my African gene pool: Dutch; East Indian (from Calcutta); German (from Saxony) and finally the universal travellers - the Scots (yes I am entitled to wear the Simpson tartan but that would raise too many questions).

It is interesting to note that both traditional Africans and the Hindus believe in reincarnation.

Guyana is the only English-speaking country in South America. Despite being explained that fact people still get Ghana (West Africa) mixed up with Guyana; even directory enquiries gets these two countries mixed up when attempting to get the telephone numbers for their respective embassies.

I was unprepared for the culture shock of living in Guyana. Firstly, Guyana was a third world country so we saw absolute poverty, as opposed to the relative poverty seen in the UK at the time. In addition, there were differing cultural attitudes; attitudes towards death being one. Guyana was more ethnically mixed and somehow the British had not eradicated these other cultures but rather embraced them in a folder marked British West Indian.

In those days, we had no television, as the size of the rivers represented barriers to transmission. The entire country relied on transmissions from two radio stations - Guyana Broadcasting Services (GBS) or Radio Demerara.

I was coming up to my tenth birthday in a very strange land and missed 'Dear Old Blighty' badly and we had no TV! Guyana always had a touch of Tennessee Williams plays about it. The land felt old and ancestral but not the stiff old and dead ancestors of England. Our ancestors felt more like we could catch a glimpse of them out of the corner of our eyes. It was a strange place, where ghosts could be seen at noon which may have to do with the high atmospheric humidity (70%), as water has a significant role in death rites in the African Traditional Religions (ATRs). The high humidity and costal daytime and nocturnal temperatures averaging 32°C and 24°C respectively make for an obscenely vibrant place where life teems in a visible manner. However, the high temperatures and humidity also make for a general feeling of oppression and always made me think of those great Tennessee Williams screenplays that I watched as kid (whether or not I fully understand the subtext of such greats as *Cat on a Hot Tin Roof*) where introspective families inexorably tore themselves apart over some scarcely-concealed scandal. There was also what I would call the legacy of disconnection as most of us had no chance of tracing our ancestors back many generations:

- The East Indians predominantly came as indentured workers who were not far above slaves (regardless of what they thought);

- The Africans came as slaves and the slaves' records were destroyed;

- The Europeans came as indentured workers or just working class folk who were nothing like our modern working class;

- The Amerindians were consistently denigrated or ignored and did not have systems of recording family histories for genealogical research.

In fact the Amerindians are the most oppressed of all people. We play a neo-colonial lip service to their full participation but they still get a bad deal.

The Guyanese author Edgar Mittleholzer (1909 to 1969) to my mind best dramatised the unfolding Amerindian emancipation and social upheavals in his trilogy of novels, *Kaywana*. In the sixties and seventies these books were unfortunately given the suggestive covers of the *Mandingo* subgenre of crude interracial eroticism but are a completely different and unique narrative.

Edgar Mittleholzer is considered the first West Indian author of international status. The fact that he took his life in Farnham in Surrey in the particularly spectacular method of self immolation, further cements my view that eventually he succumbed to the pervading insanity that tainted the country and hence exited in a highly ritualistic way. I cannot tell what drove him to commit suicide but a question that was thrust upon him from an early age was that of his skin-colour and therefore his place in the world. This issue of racial identity was made poignant, as he was mixed race but very swarthy and born into an almost white family. When he went on a pilgrimage to his ancestral area of Saxony he was met with racial hostility as opposed to being treated as a long distant relative.

With hindsight, it was clear that my return to Guyana and my culture shock was to coincide with a decade of major social upheaval.

As a boy studying for my Common Entrance Exams, I was taught that one pound was equal to four Guyanese dollars and eighty cents. Ten years later we had gotten rid of cents as they were virtually useless and one pound was worth three hundred Guyanese dollars. On top of the financial collapse, Black Power swept the Caribbean which for countries like Trinidad and Guyana with a near equal split of people of African and East Indian descent and a shameful history of racial violence was an explosive mix.

Most of the country had dark skies, as the expensive craze for extravagant lighting had not caught on. Power was expensive, as we had to import fuel oil as we had no oil reserves of our own. In fact, the blackouts that plagued the country due to the high cost of oil and wide scale mismanagement during the 1970s just further added to the darkness. Viewing the Milky Way was the norm and not the exception as it is in the UK.

Every weekday at 9PM, just as I was going to bed, there was some creepy organ music from the radio, which was tuned to Radio Demerara without fail, and the Death Announcements Programme would start. I could only describe this music as a cross between the hammy old organ of Vincent Price's 'Dr Phibes' crossed with a bit of dirge like bagpipe music.

I just could not get my head around death announcements. The adults in my extended family (including my maternal Grandmother) would listen raptly to these 15 minutes of announcements of who had died that day. The information would often include the date, time and location of the funeral. The surviving family members and even the play name (a nickname) of the deceased would also be read out. I found this odd but knew that this practice was occurring in every single household across the country. I filed it away as something that adults did and adults were a perplexing breed to me. It was inevitable that my parents would have to attend a funeral or two. In fact, as I walked around Georgetown and the East Bank of the Demerara river there was always a funeral going on.

The other thing about Guyana was the extended family that made large funerals a possibility. Even when the mass exodus out of the country occurred in the 1970s, funerals were still public affairs never to be shut in for private grief only.

I lived across the road opposite to an East Indian burial ground when we first moved back so I saw several Moslem funerals, which seemed a bit more upbeat. There were several sandbox trees and even a silk cotton tree in that cemetery which, given their folkloric wisdom of being associated with jumbies, meant no one went there after dusk despite the place being wide open.

Guyanese loved a good jumbie story. Jumbies was the colloquial Dutch word for ghosts. Guyana was once a Dutch slave colony. Wherever the word Jumbie is seen in the Caribbean it is reasonable to assume that that country was a Dutch Colony at one time. The Dutch had quite an impact on our civil engineering and left us many words like *koker* (sluice gate), and *Polder* (a reclaimed area of land from the sea). We also had a host of Dutch names like *Kykoverall*, *New Amsterdam*, *Vreed en Hoop* and *Snoek* (an ugly food fish with a long mouth).

In 1955 Edgar Mittleholzer wrote a brilliant ghost story novel along the lines of MR James entitled "My Bones and My Flute". The story is clever but scary as it has a dialogue between a slave owner killed during an uprising with a modern Guyanese family. It also captures the ambiguity of death in the Caribbean way of life.

The slave owners are alleged to have the habit (attributed to the Dutch primarily) of killing and burying the slaves with their owner's casks of gold to have them protect it in eternity. I do not know whether this was really done or maybe they sought merely to restrict the knowledge as to the precise location of the treasure. Anyway, the country had many legends of where such treasures were buried.

One day, as a young man, my maternal grandfather fell into a light sleep and dreamt that a slave came to him and told him that he was going to show him where some gold was buried as he would throw a stone and where it landed would mark the spot he should dig. Now my grandfather did wake up shortly after and saw a stone fall before his very eyes. My grandfather 'sucked his teeth 'and went into the house. I was never able to work out where the stone must have fallen in the backyard. 'Sucking one's teeth' is a general act of extreme disdain in the English-speaking Caribbean.

Jumbies were also said to be able to shade themselves under mushrooms and toadstools hence such fungi were called "Jumbie Umbrella". Jumbie Umbrella could reflect the fact that as a nation we are terrified of being poisoned so perhaps eating fungi would turn us into Jumbie – i.e. die or maybe see jumbies, as a side effect of a hallucinogenic mushroom trip.

Interestingly the East Indians of Guyana had a legend of a female entity called a Churai. The Churai was once a once a woman (presumably of

East Indian descent) who died during child birth. Now it is to be remembered that infant mortality rates and deaths during childbirth in Guyana are considerably higher than that in developed countries, and the life expectancy considerably less. The only other thing I remember about the Churia is that she was said to be able to fly; which resonates with the Semitic Lilith.

Any discussion of Jumbies and any other supernatural entities leads to considering the role of Obeah in Guyanese society. Obeah is a form of folk magic but is a mixture of Western magic and local elements. To me the influence is weak and almost non-existent. So I only mention it here to clarify the absence. Again it is the ascendency of The Great Hoax that has precluded the development of Obeah rituals that acknowledge the dead in Guyana. The etymology of Obeah has never seemed valid, however what I have seen of it in Guyana does not seem to acknowledge the dead in the way that Palo Mayombe or Lukumi does. There is certainly no spiritism, as per Kardec, the Fox Sisters or the espiritisimo of Latin America but then I have not made an academic study of Obeah practices.

When one has extended family it is inevitable that someone will die and we would be expected to do our bit. The day finally came (within six months of our return) when we had to attend a family funeral. Some ancient cousin twice removed had died. There we found ourselves in the hot sun with Dad, my brother and I in dark trousers, crisply ironed white shirts (well before the sweat soaked them) and polished black shoes (shoe polishing was my chore). Mum was in her special black dress and hat. When we were kids we had to ensure that our legs were creamed and not the ashy black of uncared for children. We trooped into church and we tried to raise the roof (and the dead) by singing at the top of our voices. I was in the school choir so did my bit and continued to do so before the hormones caught up with me. The whole place sang as one. Every hymn was belted out as opposed to the polite and muted noises I have seen in most of the mainstream UK churches. All hymns were British traditional ones. I remember *Rock of Ages* and *Abide with Me* brings a child's poignant remembering. I still have a dislike of lilies, as I associated them with funerals – especially the white ones; however I do not think that we had them much in Guyana. Funerals were large and of course, if you knew the people you had to attend. No one waited to be invited. It was the done thing to attend and be seen to be paying your respects. We never thought to analyse our blind attendance.

The high number of funerals I went to changed my perspective. I remember being at someone's funeral and watching my Dad who had stepped in as a pallbearer, as the planned person could not attend and thinking that one day I would be a big man like my dad and just step up and do that. Another time I noticed the slow march of a policeman's funeral and later became quite pleased when I mastered that aspect of drill, as an Army Reservist doing National Service.

We seemed to embrace death in a way that people in the developed West do not. Most of us kept livestock or had family that did. You could hear roosters crowing at all hours of the day and night, even in the residential areas of Bellaire and Republic Park. Chickens were killed before our eyes, cleaned and then cooked. Most men wanted to hunt as they had grown up as boys with a slingshot (catapult) that was used to terrorise the local bird life, as we rarely hit anything. Our markets heaved with live chickens and ducks that were sold for the pot. Pre-killed shrink wrapped birds were a new innovation for those who were rich and lived in 'town'.

Every house had at least one dog ostensibly to guard the house from *Tief man* (burglars); said dogs often ran out and got run over where they were left in the roadside or thrown into a ubiquitous canal where they bloated and could be seen jerking as the fish tugged at them.

Decades later in early 2007, I was working for a global company as a finance professional. I offered to go to Port Harcourt in Nigeria to retrieve a sum of money that one of our Branches had refused to return. My boss was outraged and informed me that he could not send me to Nigeria, as that is the place where, 'dead dogs are just left lying in the street'. I did not take the debate forward as it was not my personal money anyway but where did he think I had spent my formative years? Luckily for the company's bank account I engineered a coup in the branch and we got our money back.

During the mid 70s to late 80s we the citizen's of the World's First Cooperative Republic – as so claimed by our Comrade Leader and President for Life, decided to initiate a system of National Service for all eligible Guyanese nationals. I attended one of the two boys' schools that were most likely to generate the next generation of neo-colonial thieves, rapists and murderers. We found ourselves drafted into the Military Reserves. The number one murder suspect in the murder of Dr Walter Rodney went to my school (but was in a higher year to me) which was no coincidence.

Whilst in my second year of secondary school I experienced an event that I will take with me to my grave.

We were in the French lesson, which was a single period. Our teacher was Mr Pryor Jonas. Pryor was a cricket enthusiast and knew my Dad (as did half of Guyana, or so I thought).

The event happened around the first ten minutes of the 45-minute class. Pryor asked us, 'When do you become a man?'

Posing that question to a class of thirty boys who were in their early teens was possibly not a good idea. Sublime, ridiculous and thinly veiled sexual answers abounded. Still, Pryor kept repeating the question. Now school legend had it that Pryor had gone mad during an assembly but I could not ever verify this. The whole class was in an uproar towards the end of the lesson, as no French was taught on that day and the question became tantalising. Within the last minutes of the class, Pryor gave us the answer, which I am not going to tell any reader (lol).

According to Pryor, a boy becomes a man when his mother dies. I find this quite profound and very moving. Despite my reducing and increasingly grey hair; I am glad to say that according to Pryor, I am still a boy.

National Service served a number of convenient functions, the most obvious of which was to defend the country against a possible Venezuelan invasion, as there was a disputed area of land (approximately five-eighths of the country) bounded by the Orinoco and Essequibo rivers that Venezuela laid claim to in an aggressive manner. Anyway,

Comrade Leader (and thief) had attended my school back in the day so it was with obscene haste that our school cadet corp., of which I was a proud member, was inducted into "G" company of the Guyana Defence Force Reserves.

Remembrance Day was the biggest military parade in Guyana. It was made even more poignant by an old woman who always laid a doll at the foot of the Cenotaph in Georgetown. The woman in question (Mrs Merriman) had five sons who all signed up to go and fight in WW2. They all boarded the boat to the UK, which, was sunk by a German Submarine in the Atlantic. All five boys perished. This must have occurred during the early part of the war as I am informed the practice changed during the war as they split up siblings to reduce the risk of whole offspring being wiped out at one go. There was I, boots 'bulbed', and puttees tight and brasses shined, marching with the other reservists as we grimly decided to endure National Service.

Even reference was made to death in calypso. One of which was very clever as it managed to work in at least two funeral hymns.

It started like this…

A drunk man walk innna grave yard an to the top of he voice start singing out hard… Of course he was singing to his deceased friend, and so continued

well mi friend I mus' tell you how I am happy since you dead an' gone ah never out of money. I always used to tell you about your brains…

Later on the calypso managed to work in the *Abide with Me* melody, also that of *Rock of Ages* as well as another funeral hymn, but I am reminiscing of over 35 year ago.

Like all calypsos, it was a mix of teasing and acute social observation. The teasing was always humorous. It finished

Deeep in my soulllllllll, I hear my saviour call. Oh calling me. Oh calliiinnnngg meaa.

Deep in my soul no more rum for me. no rum for meeeeee. No Rum for Meeeeeeee!

Rum was the national drink and beer was for naughty women and boys who could not face rum.

Funerals had their own grim humour. Death could bring out the trickster. At one funeral the wife of the deceased put on such a show of grief that a male voice hissed, *"all she lef fe do is to jump in the grave and lie pon him"*, (make your own translation). And another voice whispered, *"Is a pity she nevah do dat when him was alive!"* which generated much ribald laughter.

We of African descent also poured libations. Many East Indians also came to do so. I watched fascinated, as Dad would pour a little splash of the first of a freshly opened bottle of rum onto the concrete of the patio or directly upon the ground for the ancestors.

My maternal grandmother and my mother got into one of the ghastly feuds that some Caribbean families seem prone to; I was angry with my grandmother as she seemed to have favourites and seemed adept at upsetting my mother. The feud lasted for several years.

Returning to the UK

I returned to live in a new UK in 1974 to follow academic aspirations, after being away for just over 5 years. Upon my return, a friend and fellow Venture Scout died in a car crash. I received a written invitation to the funeral! I had never ever received an invitation to a funeral and I was shocked. Was this a class situation or a cultural one?

The funeral was a quiet affair. It was very sad. I wondered where everyone that had known him was. Couldn't some people take time off work? It was the 1970s and people were taking time off for everything. I just did not understand why the attitude was different to the Caribbean. Maybe twenty five people attended this young man's funeral which was to my mind a poor show on the part of the living.

Twelve years after I left Guyana I had to return to the country of my birth; not only was I a man, I was a big man. Within five minutes of meeting my Dad, he asked whether I brought a white shirt and dark pants. We had a funeral to attend! I also had shoe polish and black leather brogues- so I was obviously prepared! It was the bad times when a corrupt government was draining a potentially rich country in a truly cavalier manner. Death announcements had extended to hourly programmes with urgent messages that those separated by savannah, mighty rivers and swamps came to rely on. Even our old foe of malaria and black water fever had returned to Georgetown, the capital.

During the late 1980s my maternal grandmother became very sick whilst we lived in the UK. As she took ill suddenly, I could not afford to fly back but my mother did. They had not formally resolved the animosity that arose when they both lived in Guyana but my mother was glad that she was able to see her and actually closed her eyes when she passed. With death, all arguments are forgotten. It was only later that I was told that the arguments sprang from the class structure of the Caribbean, which has proved to be a Western import that survived the "Black Power" era and has never been challenged. Another cause of ruction was that my mum dared to take my Grandmother's favourite grandchild (i.e. me) away when she went to England. I was never aware that she was particularly fond of me and she seemed to favour two of my cousins who were orphaned girls. I was just happy to be running around during my boyhood and early teens. On her deathbed she did ask my mother whether I had travelled with her to come and see her. She seemed to have clear views as to who she wanted to see around her. I did not know that she held me in such esteem but have since made my peace with her. She has pride of place on my ancestral shrine, as she has been the one that has stood up during my initiation as a Lukumi priest and has been the closest ancestor to me.

Liverpool 2011

I wrote the above article and then put it down as I felt, in an unspecified way, that it was unfinished. I was working in Liverpool's City centre over the summer and went to a bar that served food for lunch. I had noticed the bar and tariff earlier in the week and it had registered as a possibly cheap and cheerful place to eat. The bar was actually a converted pub-like space and was ordinary. The bar person politely informed me that there was a private booking on that day but I was welcome to come back the following day.

A few hours later that day, I passed the bar on my way to another venue and saw what was going on. It was a funeral celebration of the old working class type. There were a lot of people there; some of these were out on the pavement and enjoying the summer sunshine. The women wore black and the men wore dark suits or just dark trousers and white shirts. A few had turned up in jeans but it was a good turnout. Most of the men appeared to be without suits. Some of them looked of Irish descent but the important thing was that they (to my mind) represented the missing link in this article - THEY WERE WORKING CLASS!

It seems strange that it was a class analysis that was the missing element in this article on death but there you have it. There were the elements of the Caribbean funeral transported to Liverpool City centre. Everyone made an effort to attend and pay their respects by attending and dressing appropriately. My experiences in the Caribbean were of the working class or those who were a generation or two away from it at most. The funny thing is that the middle classes in any developing country, for all their posturing, cannot be equated to the middle classes from a developed country in the same way that a four star hotel in a developed country cannot be equated to that of a developing country. Both grades are relative.

A death brought everyone together but there was also a celebration of life. The young men and boys still looked vaguely uncomfortable, as perhaps shoes pinched; shirts were a bit too big or trousers not quite right. Or, maybe because there was the element of social awkwardness that I have also felt in the past. I saw one little boy got a bit too boisterous and earned the sort of stare that my father was expert at delivering.

That stare informed the boy it was better to calm down or risk the belt or just a few slaps. Happily, the boy read the stare correctly and calmed down a bit. There was a bit of laughter that lifted the warm summer afternoon and the bright sunshine seemed to have reduced the idea of human mortality at least to me a mere bystander in this important community event. These white people made me nostalgic for the Caribbean of my youth.

Had I truly forgotten about the working class? Or was it that the colonial ties between the UK and the Caribbean forged the consciousness of the "People's Republic of Guyana"? Perhaps I was just taken up with the act of writing and had merely forgotten. Anyway I had my missing link which leads me to another consideration.

There does seem to be contempt against the white working class especially the men and this contempt has led to The Great White Hoax. The enlightened middle classes who know so much, but frankly value so little by way of community have driven The Hoax. Sadly all the chattering class ever seems to do is pursue the endless task of this year's hipness. Their humanitarianism also hides an innate soulnessness that they seek to spread to everywhere they contact. Never content to simply let be, they for all their manners seem to have taken Kipling's white man's burden to mean attacking, lampooning and vilifying the working class in their own country whilst lauding extra virgin olive oils, and coffees picked by working class people of other countries. The trouble is that the working class institutions are largely long gone.

Meanwhile many of us have forgotten how to be and many do not know how to observe the passing of a loved one. In this country of plenty many must look to the so called ethnic minorities or their foreign relatives to learn how to negotiate important changes in our lives like death. Whilst the ethnic minorities lose a bit of their culture every day as they strive to become middle class.

Final thoughts

The dead are an important aspect of the living. I chose to offer my opinions as viewed through the dual lenses of the West Indies as well as the modern British viewpoint. The reason behind the social and autobiographic approach is to gently open the way for the reader to start making their own connections to their dead and perhaps shift their current framework without my ritual dogma.

I feel that during its rebirth, 20th-century magic hamstrung itself by seeking to avoid the Fraudulent Mediums Act of 1951, which was only repealed on the 28th May 2008. Given the opprobrium heaped on ritual and ceremonial magic by people who did not have a clue about it (nor had the decency to find out before engaging their mouths) it is hardly surprising that experienced practitioners of the magical arts would not be keen to publicise their exploration of such territory.

Despite our efforts the dead are with us whether we want them to be or not; either as named individuals or as the great nameless body of the dead we called Kalunga in Palo Mayombe or Los Muertos in Lukumi.

The Book of Gates: A prose arrangement
© Mogg Morgan

To be read during the twelve hours of the night. The journey through the mountains of the East and West is something achievable in life and indeed at death. If the latter then these lines could be used during the long night before the internment, perhaps over the coffin of the deceased or perhaps a death mask or photograph (its modern equivalent).

You who came into being from Re, from his Glorious Eye.
Granted to you is a hidden seat in the Desert,

Come together all those created by the gods.
The God has taken your measure in the Necropolis.

Illustration: The sun either side of mountains of death. Amratean (Nagada I) preformal period c4000 BCE

As he does for all those living on this Earth;
created as it is, from his right eye, the sun.

"The desert is bright, I give it light
With what is in me.

Souls of the West, those who would destroy humanity,
my glorious Eye is on you.

I have ordered the destruction, destruction of the enemies of Ra;
of the enemies of those upon the earth, where the chosen ones are.

Breath be given to you, among whom I am
Let there be rays for you, dweller in the *region of offerings*.

To you is restored the diadem in the desert.
To you is restored the diadem in the necropolis.

The gods shall say: "Your presence is commanded by the great god,
He who lifts up his arms and moves his legs; as shall you,

Come to us, you who share his essence; and say
Hail to the One in His disk, Great God with numerous forms."

1st Gate

At the first gate, a large serpent stands
His name "guardian of the desert" is upon the door.

He opens for Ra, and those upon the earth,

Full with the chosen ones of the gods

Your mind as a god speaks, from the prow of the sun-boat
Saying to the wise serpent: "Guardian of the Desert,

Open the Netherworld for Ra,
Open the door for the *One of the Horizon.*
The Hidden Chamber is in darkness. Waiting for him to create his forms anew.

You and the God sail through
On the winding waterway
The great door closes after you
which makes the dead souls wail.

2nd Gate
Sentiments drift, an hour already, floating in the Hidden Chamber
You are at the second gate of the night, guarded by the wise serpent

The one called "The encircler", "Open the gate" Call the gods
"For the One of the Horizon, has arrived; throw open the door

For those who are in heaven, Hail, come, let them pass
travelling in the west. "Open the door" my mind says:

"Open the door for Ra,
throw open the door for the One of the Horizon,
where he lightens the complete darkness, and makes the Hidden Chambers bright.

You and the God sail through
On the winding waterway
The great door closes after you
which makes the dead souls wail.

3rd Gate

The great serpent of time unravels, the hours before, the hours to come,
The trembling centre of the Earth, where earthquakes live

A hungry ghost, slipping deeper, deeper in the primal waters,
An ocean of souls, a sea of story, folding and unfolding before & after

Mistress of food is the name on the gate, she opens the earth
guarded by the spitting cobras, those who light for Ra, the sun god.

The gods say, "You have opened the earth,
You have opened the door, O Heavenly One."

Ra uncovers those who are in darkness,
Hail, Sun god, come to us"
Mind says to Serpent, stinging one who sits upon the gate
Open for Ra, throw open the Netherworld for the One of the Horizon.

While he lightens the complete darkness
and makes the Hidden Chamber bright

You and the God sail through
On the winding waterway
The great door closes after you
which makes the dead souls wail.

4th Gate

Jackals circle and prowl, on a gate called "She who acts"
Warmed by the wise serpent, Flame Face guards the door

The company of heaven say: "Let us open for Ra.
Throw open our gate for *Horus of the Horizon*."

Hail Ra, Come to us, Great God, Lord of Hidden things"
Your mind as a god speaks, from the prow of the sun god's-boat

"Open the door, open for the One of the Horizon.
Let him lighten the complete darkness
and make the Hidden Chamber bright."

You and the God sail through
On the winding waterway
The great door closes after you
which makes the dead souls wail.

5th Gate

Twelve gods stand on the outer wall, Mistress of Duration's gate
In the Judgement Hall of Osiris, Gods and goddesses call out

Come to us. He at the Head of the Horizon,

Great God, Light of the Earth
May thou open the Holy Gates,
throw wide the two mysterious Doors

In the crenulated Hall. Nine steps lead to a throne
where a sovereign weighs, your whole life in his hands.

On every step a god, Behold your life in the balance,
Through all its phases, Rising, culminating and decline

A confusion of images, Four antelope heads look down
Anubis broods, monkeys sailing, pigs flying by.

A pig shepherded by a baboon, wielding a crooked staff
Steady your heart to say:
"Never did I do any bad thing against the people"
.
You and the God sail through
On the winding waterway
The great door closes after you
which makes the dead souls wail.

6th Gate
You fair, united, through a gate called "seat of her lord"
Guarded by a Serpent, "He whose eye roves about."

Mind says: "Open the door for Ra,
throw open thy door for the One of the Horizon,
He lightens the complete darkness,

and makes the Hidden Chamber bright.
You and the God sail through
On the winding waterway
The great door closes after you
which makes the dead souls wail.

7th Gate

At the seventh gate things come together,
brightness at the end of the tunnel
All downstream to "The Brilliant One",
guarded by "Closed eyes" serpent

He is blind and cannot see you
Or anything you lack

Mind says; Open the Netherworld for Re, throw open thy door for the One of the Horizon, he lightens the complete darkness, and makes the Hidden Chamber Bright.

You and the God sail through
On the winding waterway
The great door closes after you
which makes the dead souls wail.

8th Gate:

The eighth gate is Glowing, the guardians you embrace
Your heart with emotion overflows, you remember "Flame Face"
The wise serpent is familiar
His warmth feels so good.

Open the door for Ra,
throw open the door for the One of the Horizon,
he lightens the complete darkness,
and makes the Hidden chamber bright.

You and the God sail through
On the winding waterway
The great door closes after you
Which makes the dead souls wail.

9th Gate

The ninth door is called, the Gate of Honour
Guarded by the Serpent: "Horn of the Earth"

The outgrowing of the earth, the joy of rising up
Encompassing, supporting, the life force coming back
Mind says: Open the door for Re, throw open thy door for the One of the Horizon,
He lightens the complete darkness, and makes the Hidden chamber bright.

You and the God sail through
On the winding waterway
The great door closes after you
Which makes the dead souls wail.

10th Gate

At the tenth gate, you see more on the lintel,
The company of heaven, changed to twenty four cobras

But you fear them not, the upper guardian with his knife of flint
you know his name "executioner", you are no impostor.

You have passed the lower regions, know the names of all
"The Uniter" is the wise serpent, things are coming together.

Minds says: Open the Netherworld of Ra, throw open thy door.
He lightens the complete darkness, and makes the Hidden Chamber
bright.

You and the God sail through
On the winding waterway
The great door closes after you
which makes the dead souls wail.

11th Gate

The eleventh gate is clearer still, its name "Mysterious of Approaches
Guarded by the Serpent, "The One in his discharge"

On the lintel two sceptres rest, capped by the heads
Of Father and son, Horus and Osiris.

Each wears the red crown, of the south the sceptres say:
"Peace thou whose forms are numerous,
Peace thou whose forms are numerous."

The old body is gone, cut away from you by the knives
of the cutting one, what remains is the crowned head.

Your soul is in heaven,
your body in the earth,
greatness has been ordained
by your very own self.

Mind says: "Open the Netherworld of Ra, throw open thy door.
He lightens the complete darkness, he gives light to the Chamber of
Purity (wabet).

You and the God sail through
On the winding waterway
The great door closes after you
which makes the dead souls wail.

12th Gate

After your long night, the final gate is here
"She whose power is holy", two pillars with human heads

They face each on each, Atum the setting sun
Kephra rising, coming, the beginning with the end

Through twin doors of the horizon, It is the dawn
When holy serpents fly and two cobras lie

Isis & her sister Nephthys, Those who light for Ra
going after this god, Into mysterious Door of the West,

Mind says to a serpent at the door, the *One of the Morning*,
You who open for Ra. "Open the gate,

throw open the door, for the One of the Horizon,
for he comes out of the mysterious region, to rest upon the body of Nuit.

Minds says to the *Encircler*, You upon the door:
"Open the gate for Ra, open for the One of the Horizon,

for he comes out of the mysterious region,
to move over the body of Nuit."

You and the God sail through
On the winding waterway
The great door closes one last time
which makes the dead souls wail.

Come out into the light, and contemplate death and birth
The eternal sun, towed by eight gods

On the sun boat of the morning, Lifted by the Abyss
Abysmal waters surging up, from the faraway world
.
Kephra the sacred scarab,
As new sun born through eastern mountains
Isis and Nephthys bearing him up, to the waiting goddess of the sky

Who stands above earthly sphere, out of the old and into the new
You are lifted into her arms,
Mother of the gods, Nuit.

Biographies of Contributors

Michael Clarke

Michael Clarke was born in Norfolk and was educated at Norwich School and Trinity College Cambridge. For many years he has taught at Magical Moots specialising in the Folk Magic of East Anglia and the Hermetic Tradition. He has spent over twenty five years in research and experimental magical work. He has founded and directs two teaching groups.

Nevill Drury

Dr Nevill Drury is an independent researcher whose specialist interests include modern Western magic, shamanism, consciousness research and visionary art. Born in England in 1947, he has lived in Australia since he was nine years old. For many years he worked in the Australian book industry as an editor and art book publisher and in 2008 received his PhD from the University of Newcastle. He now lives on the South Coast of New South Wales and works as a full-time writer and occasional lecturer. Nevill's books have been published in 25 countries. Recent publications include *Sacred Encounters: Shamanism and Magical Journeys of the Spirit* (2003); *The Dictionary of Magic* (2005) and *Stealing Fire from Heaven: the Rise of Modern Western Magic* (2011).

Sue Fox

"I am a photographer and writer who depicts the transgressive and the taboo. I am known internationally as a photographer of the dead and have shown with Boltanksi, Peter Witkin, Serrano and Hirst. I have written six novels about art, sex, and dark minds (underpinned by the voice of the cunt). I perform my readings and do other exclusive performances, most recently working with Ron Athey in 'Gifts of the Spirit' - in automated writings/séance and hypnosis set. I am a pig clown in an extreme art clown troupe. I am publishing my first novel this year via Paraphilia.

I like to make people think and wake them up to be fully alive. I like to rip their heads off with words and hardcore images. I create series of work like fountainbleu to explore the body, drugs, blood, genitalia, sex and death. I am rude and in your face. I am like a gun.

I am a film & media lecturer at MMU teaching photography. I am a great motivator to get young people to express themselves through all media. I am not your average teacher. I am into being unique and exploring boundaries. I work inside out and back to front.

My images and words remind me of barbed wire. Once you see them you get caught up and lethally bloodied. I am not for the faint hearted. My images are like tiny atom bombs going off in the heart of you. Art should be prolific, edgy, and like dynamite. Art should force you to change and irrevocably damage you. Art should be insightful, like some punk revolution. You should produce work that scars."

Sarah Grimstone

Sarah was initiated into the Ordo Astrum Serpentis in 1984. The group was an offshoot of Alex and Maxine Saunders' coven but was a little more of a left hand path order than a Wiccan coven. She has been a priestess of the Egyptian God Seth since he appeared to her in a dream in 1984. She has written for Penthouse and Minx magazine and for ten years has written under the pseudonym Grim Rita for a website called Faceparty, where she has doled out 'advice' to teenagers on subjects that would make 'Dear Deirdre' blush.

She did the London circuit as a stand-up comedian for two years, gigging three times a week until she realised 'fuck this is boring'.

She lives in London and occasionally does the odd 'Occult Comedy Comparing' at events. Someone once described this as being a bit 'niche'.

She believes that through comedy she can engage in a dialogue with the divine and feels she can achieve gnosis through this medium. 'It pisses all over meditation'.

Louise Hodgson

Louise Hodgson was born in Sussex and brought up in Cheshire. She now lives in west Dorset. She has a background in art and theatre and is currently finishing a book on the secret places of her locality. Her magical work has been influenced by working within the A.A. and T.O.P.Y, her arcane studies, contacts which shall be nameless, the landscape and the good friends within the magical community that she has met over the years.

Gerard Hutton

Gerard was born on December 17th, 1962 in the city of Bath UK, where many childhood hours passed admiring the incredible architecture of his Roman ancestors.

He grew up surrounded by the glorious English countryside and its ever changing weather, and an interest in the play of light and the patterns of the natural world was kindled. Yoga and Massage became a way of life for him in the late 1980s. He graduated as a remedial/sports massage therapist in 1995 and a yoga instructor in 2000.

In 2009 he married and relocated to the USA with his wife Kimberly, where they currently live in Connecticut.

His joy and passion for photography is the lure of the light, trying to capture the essence and spirit of nature. He believes that the image should be created in the camera at the time of shooting using whatever natural light and magic is available.

Ruth Kenyon

Brought up in the North East of England, Ruth has spent the last eleven years running libraries in various educational institutions in the London area. Staying with her partner on the Norfolk / Suffolk border has persuaded her to move East. Hopefully this will give more opportunities to photograph the area and its natural beauty.

"This the way the world ends
Not with a bang but a whimper"
           T.S. Eliot, The Hollow Men

Mishlen Linden

Mishlen Linden (http://www.mishlenlinden.com/) is a magickian, musician, artist and writer and the author of the definitive *Typhonian Terotomas* which Kenneth Grant considered to be 'too dangerous to publish'. She has been a practising Tibetan Buddhist for over 15 years.

Louis Martinie

Louis Martinie is a writer, percussionist, and drummer. He is also an Honorary Member of the Louisiana State Legislature. His books include *The New Orleans Voodoo Tarot* and he is the editor for *Black Moon Publishing*, and has been associated with the anarchistic grouping of ritual magicians known as *Bate Cabal*. Martinie is an elder and priest in The New Orleans Voodoo Temple and teaches and offers confirmation in an Order of Service to the Loa that combines elements of New Orleans Voodoo with Tibetan Buddhism.

Josephine McCarthy

Josephine McCarthy is a seasoned occultist and writer living in the wilds of the Dartmoor National Park in the UK. Josephine has taught and led various Western Mystery groups throughout the USA and UK for many years, and has written a variety of magical non-fiction and fiction. Her previous books include *The Exorcists Handbook* and *The Work of the Hierophant*.

Mogg Morgan

MMM is a senior occultist, author, publisher, commentator, theologian, historian, lecturer, teacher and researcher. Following his earlier experiences with Kenneth Grant's Typhonian OTO he has continued his own journey into the Pagan/Kemetic tradition. He shares his vision through a series of books including *Tankhem: Meditations on Seth Magick*, *The Bull of Ombos*, *Supernatural Assault in Ancient Egypt* and *The Wheel of the Year in Ancient Egypt*.

Nema

Nema encountered the works of Aleister Crowley in the early 1970s and became a member of Kenneth Grant's Typhonian Order for several years. During the same time period, she practiced group rituals with other magickians in Cincinnati, Ohio, and became a member of *Bate Cabal*, publisher of the *Cincinnati Journal of Ceremonial Magick*.

Nema is an experienced magickian and mystic, and the author of *Maat Magick: a Guide to Self-Initiation; The Way of Mystery: Magick, Mysticism & Self-Transcendence; The Priesthood: Parameters and Responsibilities*, and other writings.

She is an Elder and High Priestess of the Circle of the Sacred Grove, Church of Pantheist Wicca, and an initiate of Adi Nath Tantra. She and her husband Lyrus live in south-eastern Ohio, in the foothills of the Appalachian mountains. Nema is a founding member of the Horus-Maat Lodge; information about the HML is at http://www.horusmaat.com.

Ode bi tola

Ode bi tola in Cuban Yoruba translates as, 'The Hunter brings Glory'. The 'bi' also signifies that he was the first person to be initiated to his specific Orisha (the hunter and magic deity *Ochossi*) in his then Godparent's Ile (temple) in the early 2000s in the USA.

Following the retirement of his Godparent he was also initiated in Palo Mayombe to the Santo Christo Buen Viaje Lucero Mundo Kanda (Clan).

He then further pursued his destiny by being initiated as a Babalawo in the USA. The divinations that he underwent during his Babalawo initiation confirmed and built on those of his initiation as a priest and confirm that he had a facility for speaking and working with the dead.

Ode was initiated to western magic a few months after his 18th birthday having responded to a small advert in the back of Marian Green's 'Green Circle magazine'. He diligently applied himself to the entrance ordeals and thence to his magical studies. He also found time to write articles for Chris Bray's *Lamp of Thoth* Magazine under a variety of pseudonyms as he was trained in the full range of Western Magic and has also contributed to Charlotte Rodgers' 'The Bloody Sacrifice'.

Ode is in his early fifties and lives in the North of England where he works as a commercial chartered accountant. He is still active in ritual and ceremonial magic.

John Power

John holds a Masters Degree in Jungian Psychology and Art Therapy. He has taught in schools, colleges and prisons in his own locality for over 30 years. His remaining classes are with those who are recovering from mental illness.

Like Austin Spare he has little time for the art establishment. Even Art Schools can smother, as much as foster, creativity. Educational establishments inevitably pass on mainstream values, and the role of the artist, poet and philosopher is to challenge the views of the petit bourgeoisie. So, nearing the end of his teaching career he is happy at last to become a doer, rather than a fosterer of others ideas and skills and ideas, even though this has been most enjoyable, despite the establishment.

Owing to his interest in tantrik art and philosophy he began a correspondence with Guru Mahendranath, known as Dadaji, in India, which lasted 20 years until Dadaji's health failed prior to his death. They met several times while Dadaji was still alive.

Ariadne Spyridonos Xenou

Ariadne Spyridonos Xenou was born in Athens, Greece. Her family were Greek immigrants from Asia Minor and Zanynthos. She moved to Scotland in 1998 where she got her BAHons in Photography. She completed an MPhil in the Byzantine Orthodox Visual Culture and moved on to research the visual culture of Orthodox death in Athens. Her research constitutes visual anthropology, where theories and practices of photography are always the primary tools of observing, decoding and communicating the subject matter. She just completed a practice-led PhD on Athenian thanatology under the title *A Likeness of Absence: Photography and the Contemporary Visual Culture of Death in Athens*. She is now permanently based in Edinburgh where she teaches photography and critical theory in Edinburgh Napier University.

Ariadne's journey began with Barthes' *ca-a-été* and culminates with Derrida's *we owe ourselves to death*. In between, she roams from Asia Minor, the geographical location of Byzantium and the birthplace of her mother's family, to Athens, her birthplace, the city of light and death, and from there to Edinburgh, the Athens of the North. Through this historical, cultural and predominantly photographic journey, Ariadne considers cultural representations of global and individual death. This is a personal as well as cultural story. Going through history, religion and culture, what she discovered is that the nexus of photography and death is all about the individualism of the "I" and the universality of the "eye".

Ruth Kenyon

Ruth Kenyon

Index

A
Abortion 138
Abyss 21
Africa 55, 69, 134, 151
Alchemy 68
Amerindians 152, 153
Ancestors 7, 9, 10, 21, 33, 34, 35, 38, 65, 123, 134, 151, 162
  Cults of the 10
Ancient Order of Bonesmen 129
Angelic 25, 27
Asia 55, 186
Astarte 31
Atheism 38
Atman 144
Australia 41, 55, 149, 179
Austria 124
Azazel 70

B
Ba 139
Babalawo 118, 185
Baphomet 31
Barbados 149
Bardo Chikai 77
Bardo Chonyid 85, 97, 106
Bardo Sidpa 86, 106, 107, 111, 112
Bardo Thodol 75, 77, 79, 80
Basho 117
Bat 104, 133
Bees 123
Bereaved 20, 131
Bible 123
Bird 103, 104, 112, 158
Blackmore, Dr Susan 45
Blood 56, 77, 92, 99, 101, 102, 103, 104, 108, 130, 133, 137, 180
Bodhisattva 80
Bonpo 76
Britain 41, 55, 129, 134
Buddhist 55, 72, 183
Bush, Nancy Evans 54

C
Caribbean 147, 148, 149, 154, 155, 156, 162, 163, 164, 165, 166
Catholic 13, 38, 68, 128
Caucasian 48
Cemetery 122, 155
Cernunnos 31
China 55
Christian 13, 20, 37, 38, 48, 54, 55, 124, 128, 132, 139, 145
Churai 156
Collective Unconscious 79
Conception 20, 78, 138
Consciousness 20, 21, 23, 37, 38, 39, 40, 42, 43, 45, 46, 51, 52, 56, 57, 58, 63, 70, 76, 77, 79, 85, 106, 108, 109, 110, 113, 115, 129, 140, 166, 179
Cooper, Sharon 47, 59
Corpse 102, 108, 122, 146
Crematorium 122
Crocodile 102, 104
Crow 103, 104
Cthonic 78
Cunning man 131

D
Dakini 79, 99, 100

Dalai Lama 76, 77, 140
Danse Macabre 70
Dark Goddess 19
Demeter 31, 68
Demonic 68, 133
Diana 31
Divine Consciousness 23
Divine Mother 83, 88, 93, 94, 95, 96, 97, 102
Divinity 58, 130
Dog 104, 112, 125, 159
Dorje 143
Dying 13, 18, 20, 28, 37, 38, 39, 41, 43, 50, 51, 58, 122, 141, 146

E

East Anglia 129, 179
Ecstasy 47
Egyptian 24, 67, 181
Elephant 94, 104
Eleusinian 68
England 78, 135, 149, 151, 164, 179, 182, 185
Enlightenment 80, 81, 82, 83, 84, 85, 87, 89, 90, 91, 93, 94, 95, 96, 97, 98, 101, 102, 103, 104, 105, 110, 116, 143
Espiritisimo 157
Etruscan 24
Euthanasia 118
Exorcism 20, 115

F

Father 9, 16, 17, 21, 22, 48, 112, 121, 140, 165
Folk 122, 124, 126, 127, 128, 129, 130, 152, 157
Fox 103, 104
Fraudulent Mediums Act of 1951 167
Fundamentalism 38
Funeral 57, 123, 124, 133, 145, 147, 154, 157, 158, 161, 162, 163, 165

G

Ganesh 78
Garden of Remembrance 122
Gau 141
Gautama Buddha 80
Gehinnom 38
Genetic 34
Ghost 109, 114, 125, 126, 135, 155
Goat 104
God 21, 37, 42, 50, 52, 60, 84, 86, 114, 120, 137, 181
Goetic 10
Greek 68, 69, 186
Grey, Margot 41, 46
Greyson, Dr Bruce 41, 53
Guardians 29, 30
Guyana 149, 150, 151, 153, 154, 155, 156, 157, 158, 160, 161, 163, 164, 166

H

Hades 133, 135
Hadit 32
Hapsburgs 130
Hawaii 55
Heaven 13, 21, 38, 68, 124, 139, 179
Hecate 31
Heim, Professor Albert 40
Hell 13, 15, 33, 38, 54, 68, 75, 94, 109, 110, 112, 114, 124, 125, 139
Hermes 133, 135, 136
Hieronymus Bosch 68
Hindu 55
Hitchens, Christopher 38
Homer 126, 132, 133
Horse 95, 104, 112, 123
Hungry Ghosts, Festival of 9

I

Icon 142
Inanna 31
Incarnation 138, 144
India 55, 76, 186
International Association for Near-Death Studies 41, 53
Iraq 69
Irish 33, 165
Isis 31
Islam 37, 38

J

James, Bond 117
James, Debbie 53
Judaism 23, 37
Jumbies 155, 156
Jung, Carl 79

K

Ka 139
Kabbalah 68
Kali 31
Kalunga 167
Karma 77, 79, 87, 91, 99, 102, 105, 107, 108, 109, 110, 111, 114, 116
Kellehear, Allan 55
Kerboull, Jean 147
Ketamine 45
Kipling 166
Klagweiber 124
Kletti, Ray 40
Kubler-Ross, Dr Elisabeth 41, 50, 51, 52, 59, 60

L

L.S.D 79
Last Judgement 38
Leary, Dr Timothy 57, 79
Lennon, John 79
Leopard 104
Lilith 157
Lion 69, 103, 104
Loa 64
Los Muertos 167
Lotus 96, 114, 115
Lucifer 70
Lukumi 118, 157, 164, 167

M

Magic 10, 13, 24, 28, 122, 148, 157, 167, 179, 185
Magician 13, 23, 131
Magick 76
Malkuth 21, 143
Manchester 72
Mandala 76, 77, 78, 99
Maya 68
Mediaeval 68
Memorial 122, 124
Mindsight 49
Miner Holden, Dr Janice 53
Mirror 94, 98, 108
Mittleholzer, Edgar 153, 155
Monkey 104
Moody, Dr Raymond 40, 41
Morgue 72

N

Near-death experiences 39
Necromancy 128
Nelson, Thomas 54, 60
New Orleans 66, 141, 183
New Zealand 55
Nigeria 159
Norbu, Mr. 140, 143
Noyes, Russell 40
Nuit 31
Nuns 13

O

Obeah 157
Odyssey 126, 133
OM-MANI-PADME HUM 87
On Life After Death 50, 59, 60
Orisha 118
Osiris 31

Osis, Dr Karlis 41
Out-of-the-body experiences 48
Owl 103

P
Pagan 121, 145
Palo Mayombe 157, 167, 185
Pan 31, 78
Paradise 38, 100
Parasites 25
Parnia, Dr Sam 41
Peacock Angel 70
Persephone 68
Persia 69
Possession 140
Potters Field 124
Prayer 28
Pregnancy 127, 138
Priest 146, 164, 183, 185
Priestess Miriam 66
Priests 7, 13, 118
Primary Clear Light 76, 78, 81, 89, 90, 91, 92, 105, 110, 111, 113
Protestant 38
Purgatory 13, 21, 68, 140

Q
Qlipoth 68

R
Rawlings, Dr Maurice 54
Reincarnation 13, 77, 79, 80, 150, 151
Reliquaries 129
Respiration 39
Resuscitation 40
Reynolds, Pam 56, 59
Richard, Dawkins 38
Ring, Kenneth 41, 42, 43, 47, 52, 55, 59
Rites of passage 13
Ritual 13, 21, 28, 65, 118, 131, 140, 146, 149, 167, 183, 185
Rosin, Carol 57

S
Sabom, Dr Michael 41, 43
Saints 34, 128, 133
Samsara 77, 93
Sangha 143
Scientific research 38, 50, 53
Scorpion 104
Séances 132
Sekhmet 69, 70
Serdahely, William 54
Set 70
Sexuality 33, 69, 77, 112, 113, 130, 134, 160
Shakti 28, 76, 78, 93
Sheol 38
Siva 75, 76, 78
Skull 99, 103
Snake 68, 103, 104
Soul 20, 21, 26, 27, 30, 34, 37, 40, 46, 67, 68, 71, 137, 138, 143, 145, 162
South America 55, 148, 151
Sow 103, 104
Spetzler, Dr Robert 56
Spiritualism 131
Spirituality 38
Stag 104
Star Trek 57
  Gene Roddenberry 57
Stupa 144
Sutherland, Dr Cherie 41

T
Talmud 37
Tao 28, 80, 84, 107
Taxter Rinpoche 140
Tennessee Williams 151
Thailand 55
Thanatology 39
Tibet 55, 67, 75, 76, 77, 78, 79, 141, 143, 183

Tiger 103, 104
Torah 37
Tradition 10, 76, 121, 132
Trance 140
Tree of Life 17, 21
Trinidad 154
Tunnel experiences 45, 55

U
Ultimate Reality 90, 92
Ulysses 126
Underworld 17, 19, 21, 24, 25
Uttara Kaula 76

V
Vampire 129, 130
Van Lommel, Dr Pim 41
Venezuela 160

Victorian 13
Vision 17, 18, 19, 20, 23, 24, 27, 49, 88
Voodoo Spiritual Temple 62, 66
Vulture 103, 104

W
Western Mysteries 24
Wolf 103, 104
Working class 152, 165, 166
Wotan 31
Wrathful Deity 115

Y
Yak 104
Yezedi 69
Yin and Yang 80
Yoruba 118, 184

Charlotte Rodgers
The Bloody Sacrifice
ISBN 978-1-906958-30-5, £10.99,
155pages

Charlotte Rodgers is a non denominational magickal practitioner and an animist, and The Bloody Sacrifice is the story of her work with blood. It chronicles her use of road kill and blood in art, ritualised scarification and tattoo work, and the use of venous and menstrual blood in magick. Also included are Charlotte's interviews with tattoo artists; priests from belief systems which utilise blood sacrifice; artists who use their own HIV positive blood as a medium; and those who use mortifications and body modification to effect changes in consciousness and self.

All here share a common bond of talent combined with an ability to articulate their beliefs. For example Louis Martinie, a priest in the New Orleans Voodoo Spiritual Temple. Martinie has integrated his Tibetan Buddhist beliefs into his Voodoo practice and in doing so shows how personal spiritual evolution can effect change within a syncretic religion.

As a blood related illness affected various parts of Charlotte's life, she was given a chance to explore blood ritual in a very different way. Documenting this part of her journey gives an understanding of AIDS, HIV and HCV, and its effect on spirituality and contemporary blood rites.

Blood Ritual, with all its history, baggage and dangers holds a power to create change. Whether this power is held within blood and how much impact is created merely by our perception is for the reader to decide. The Bloody Sacrifice is an honest, modern and thought provoking personal insight into an ancient aspect of our spirituality and creativity.

Order direct from
Mandrake of Oxford, PO Box 250, Oxford, OX1 1AP (UK)
Phone: 01865 243671 (for credit card sales)
Prices include economy postage
online at - www.mandrake.uk.net

Ingram Content Group UK Ltd.
Milton Keynes UK
UKHW051516140623
423358UK00016B/299